MW00781044

Bedtime Stories For Adults:

Relaxing Short Stories designed to Fully Restore your Body and Mind. Reduce Anxiety and Prevent Insomnia with Deep Sleep Hypnosis. Let Yourself Go on a Magical Journey.

Claire Watts

Table of Contents

Introduction

Bedtime stories were fun to hear. Sometimes, your parents would do voices. Other times, they'd just read the books quietly, and you'd pay attention each time. Sometimes they'd be tales you've heard plenty of times, other times they were tales they fabricated on a whim.

Regardless of what type of tales you heard, bedtime stories are wonderful for falling asleep. Most of them have soft, pleasant words that people love to hear.

Do you remember some of your former bedtime stories?

If you do, do you remember how they made you feel? The words you heard? The imagery you'd remember?

All of this plays a key role in why bedtime stories for adults are so important, and why, with each story you hear, you feel relaxed, at ease, and of course, able to sleep.

Each story will have fun, whimsical ideas, or imagery of different scenarios that you've been through before. The fun and excitement of going on a trip, the quests that you have, and even, a sleep fairy that will help you sleep. With every single story, you'll be spirited away on a wonderful adventure, one that's fun for you, and a good trip for everyone in the story.

If you have trouble falling asleep, just imagine yourself in the different scenarios each of these wonderful characters go through. As you get spirited away in this adventure, you'll notice that, with each time, and each place, it'll change for you. There are many different aspects to consider with each story, and many adventures to be had.

Also, don't think you'll hear the same story twice. While it might be the same words, there might be new adventures to be had, and new ideas that come forth.

Listening to bedtime stories will help foster your creative juices, help you improve you with ideas for the future, and also reduce stress. By listening to these ten wonderful stories, you'll be able to fall asleep soundly, and you'll be amazed at how refreshed you feel whenever you wake up.

Bedtime stories for adults also help with taking your attention off the troubles of life. If you're an adult, chances are you have some kind of stress. Whether it be work, bills, or even your family that stress adds up and it can make it hard for you to fall asleep. Many adults suffer from insomnia or can only sleep for a certain period of hours. That combined with the incredibly long work weeks, and also with the early morning shifts, it's not easy out there. But, with these bedtime stories, you'll relax your mind, you'll take your attention off the troubles you have, and promote relaxation, and of course sleep with each word you hear.

Many adults benefit from these types of stories. Some of us might wonder why, but if you take a moment to think about it, when was the last time you weren't focused on the stresses at hand, but instead on a relaxing, fun bedtime story that will help with sleep. If you can't remember, then you need these bedtime stories for adults.

With each story, each word uttered, each sound you hear, I hope they will lull you to sleep. It helps as well with shutting off your brain, helping you get focused on the different words you hear, and instead of feeling stressed and depressed, you'll get your mind off the troubles you have, and instead, feel brighter than ever.

So, sit back, get comfortable, and listen to these relaxing bedtime stories. And with every one of these, you'll feel yourself whisked away into the tales they tell, and hopefully, you'll have pleasant dreams and a wonderful sleep as you continue to hear each story, and the creative, relaxing, and inspiring tales each one of them has to offer.

The stories contained here were written for two purposes: for your enjoyment or for the enjoyment of the person you are reading them to, and to help you start to fall asleep better at night and wake up feeling fully rested. When I say they will help you achieve deeper states in the unconscious, what I am really talking about is mindfulness. I am sure you have heard this word before, but perhaps you do not know what it means or how to practice it.

You may wonder how stories fit into the picture of mindfulness, anxiety treatment, and insomnia. The reason stories help us fall asleep is because we need to fall deep into our unconscious mind to make ourselves fall asleep.

These stories will manifest in your mind as larger-than-life environments and calming descriptions of beauty. Reading them will encourage your brain to use your unconscious mind to imagine these scenarios and truly put yourself in them and experience their beauty and tranquility. It won't take long before you let go of the real world completely and become lost in the visceral lands you explore. You will find yourself waking up the next day feeling fully rested.

Chapter1: Night Dream

"If you are that worn outside, then head to bed," mum said. And that I really did, even though Darkness did not come back yet out my window. My arms were so weak I could not get off my socks. They kept sticking with my toes. I crawled under the covers. When I am very exhausted, I fantasize...

...that I must visit the bank for some cash. Dad's birthday is tomorrow. And I would like to buy him something super-duper unique.

"Hurry," mother said, "until the bank closes" She constantly reminds me I've my own cash. Occasionally I overlook my bankbook states I have $36 bucks left. The bus driver is quite fine when I inform him I don't have any cash. "However, I will pay you back once I get some in the lender," I state.

We journey down busy roads, beyond tall buildings and I leap off the three Steps in the bus. There's a very long line of folks in the bank. Along with also the Teller's wicket seems like it's a mile off. So I rely on bushels of butterflies while waiting. Ultimately it is my turn. And I appear at this guy behind the countertop. He has to be eight feet tall. Initially I thought that he was really wonderful.

"There is no money here for you," he explained. "You should have spent it all."

"But...however, my mom said there are a few left," I replied. "I stored it all Myself from my newspaper route."

"Then you must check with her," said the man sternly. "Or you have to arrive at the wrong lender," he explained, displaying his teeth.

I looked into his eyes again. And watched his grin. Was he faking for a sly coyote? Last summer I found you at a field near my property. The creature appeared doomed with his hairy tail.

On the way home I met a great woman. When I told her the sad story, " she felt sorry for me. She should have been wealthy because she gave me an entire bag full of cash. I could not take all of it. I gave her a pile of paper cash. If she had to purchase a bag of fries, or visit a picture.

I do not need to move home. I've got enough cash for an Amazing present for my dad. "Something very unique," I mentioned to a white bunny, sitting on the chair beside me. I believe he's after me home.

"You're careful, the coyote does not attempt to consume you," I state. I show him teeth. However, it does not frighten him.

Round the corner, there's a small girl standing on the pavement. I get off the bus to determine why she's crying. "My hands are cold," she explained. I bought her a pair of red mittens. She's so amazed she dared to thank me personally.

Now I'm hungry, and exhausted. I sit down on the sidewalk and start my Birthday present knapsack. There's half an apple sliced sandwich, and 2 chocolate chip cookies. Shortly my knapsack is vacant, except for a single crust. It attempts to hide from the corner.

"If I had a blueberry jam," I told the bus driver awaiting me. "It could be yummy with this crust of bread"

"I will take you to where blueberries are big. And succulent," he explained.

The bus brought me away in town, and over a crowded highway. Even beyond fishing boats at the harbor. Subsequently the bus turned up a gravel street. I observed a pheasant hurry throughout the street. We moved beyond fields of hay along with a large mountain, and we eventually ceased. The bus had a flat tire.

I got off and appeared in a valley full of blueberries. And awaiting beside the very first bush was the white bunny. "How can he find me?" I wondered.

I immediately filled my knapsack with succulent berries. My palms look like they are painted blue. And that my back is tired of bending over a lot. I sat on a log and also removed my shoe and sock. Then I started to shout. I had been fearful the coyote could return and bite my fur.

What exactly was I doing here? I believed. There aren't any presents for daddy. Besides, that sly coyote may find me. After conducting just like thunder throughout a subject I tripped over a log. Then fell to a tiny creek, using squishy mud. Was something pursuing me? Perhaps it was white bunny. I shook myself tender, how my friend's pet does. Spotty is his title. I mean that is the puppy's name. I discovered more yelling. However, it seemed far off. My eyes were shut tightly. The same as the front door once I slam it.

...Subsequently I open my eyes one at a time. Mother and dad are looking at me. The kitty is on my bed. And I am too. While I look from the window, then the coyote's face is not there. And He's laughing. I chased my mom. She starts to laugh also. Oh...Oh. I forgot to Get Dad's current. Close my eyes and rush back to my own dreaming.

Chapter2: A Hike in the Forest

You had overheard someone at a local café talking about a strange and secluded place less than an hour up into the mountains that is relatively untouched by man, a slight miracle, and totally accessible. You have the day off, so you decide to go and see it for yourself. The drive there is strangely serene. This must be a day that a lot of people decided to stay indoors, because there is almost no traffic on the roads, becoming less and less as you go further up the mountain roads. The weather is just right, not too hot and just a little bit cool. You decide not to listen to any music on your trip, as you feel it would only distract you from yourself, and you feel very comfortable with yourself right now. Outside your car windows, the density of the trees increases, making it harder and harder to recognize where one tree begins and the other ends. Eventually, you are in a sea of green, bleeding into an infinite blue sea above it. You begin to feel totally grounded yet totally enlightened, your feet on the ground yet your head in the clouds. You've forgotten that you are even driving by the time you get to your destination. You step out of your car and you feel like you've been there all along. The trailhead is incredibly esoteric, yet totally and naturally definite, as if the trees have made their own way just for you to progress. You don't even remember what it was that signified to you that this is where you were heading, no sign that you recall having seen, yet you took just the right turn and ended up exactly where you wanted to be. A couple of feet further down the way, and your car disappears from your sight, and you are totally entrenched in a brown and green void that you seem to be directly in the middle of. The tops of the trees seem to make a sky in their own right, and the blue sky above them seems to be a more ethereal divine abyss beyond this. Immediately, wildlife begins to bristle all around you. Each tree, and there are thousands, spread infinitely, is alive, it seems, with its own colony of critters, scurrying up and down the shafts of the trees where they blend into the vast array of birds fluttering to and fro across each tree top. Deer cross your path without a second thought, as if you are nothing to them but another tree among the infinite. You do not disrupt them. Each and every green patch among the endless dirt is bristling, and you know that each one houses its own infinite array of life, from the visible to the microscopic. Each speck of dirty is alive with more life than you can possibly see. The sounds of all this life together form a grand orchestral score, with the percussion of the breeze against the limbs of the trees and the greenery being its ephemeral skeleton. There are the violas and violins of the chirping birds making their own independent songs, and the soft and expressive squeaks of the chipmunks and squirrels and smaller things tied to the ground. There are the cellos of the four-legged herbivores, close and off in the distance, communicating to each other in a language you cannot understand literally but feel a close relationship to in some way intangible to your own waking experience. And, off in the distance, there are the bass growls of the grand beasts that hide in the shadows, far away from you, giving you your space as you give them theirs. All the while, your footsteps against the grass and the dirt and the leaves and the twigs form their own accouterment to this vast symphony, a tiny little dance in a great and grand field, tying everything together. You stop for a second and hold your hands out, and into your palms from a connective embrace with this infinite multitude of life before and behind and above you. All this, you are a part of, as it is a part of you, the natural order of things, the earth and the sky and the dirt and below. Above and below, the life that expands infinitely outwards. You feel totally whole in this vast open nature, and for a moment you just stand in its existence, a part of it. Then you move on. Further and further down the trail, the wilderness growing denser and denser as the treetops close in on the skies above them, the light become scanter and scanter as if to pay its respects to the exponentially growing depths of this wide-spreading forest. Eventually, you are no longer sure if it is night or day, but everything is awake, and you can see it all. The earth glows and radiates into you with ancient and uncompromising power. You cannot believe that before, in this same day, you were among men in their cities, at the café, overhearing about this strange and magical place. Somehow, these two worlds exist as one. Yet you are here, now, and feel as if you always have been, and as if the world of the city had never really existed. There was only this, just you, and this infinite nature at your fingertips, and you at its. In the close distance there is a glowing light, and you begin to hear the sounds of rushing water growing stronger and stronger. This sound and sight is accompanied by a cool, moist feeling in the air, as if an ancient spirit is welcoming you into its embrace, and you are being swallowed by its presence as if into the belly of a great whale. This entrance becomes closer and closer, and you feel yourself being overtaken by the golden light emanating so thoroughly defined through this infinite abyss of dark, deep wilderness you have found yourself in the midst of. You slowly but surely make your way, as the sound of the water becomes almost all there is, drowning out so beautifully the choir of the mountains, as you transcend that golden light and find yourself in the valley of a great and roaring river, starting from one eternity and going into the next, farther and farther each way then the eye could ever see. It is day; there can be no doubt, and the brightest, purest day you could ever imagine. The sky is the bluest it has ever been; as if all the air that has ever existed has parted its way for you to totally connect to the sun, straight through the atmosphere. The sight and the sound totally overtakes you, and you feel for a moment as if you are a planet unto yourself, hurtling at the speed of light through space, yet totally and serenely still, and totally alone yet loved in the abyss of the universe. You realize, here, now, it is your time to rest. You sit down, and for a long time, maybe years, you stare at the river rushing forward through time, on and on, forever. Nighttime comes, and goes, and comes, and goes, and the river never stops. You feel as if you have entered an eternal hibernation, having totally melded your consciousness with the vast and flowing river, and the infinite wilderness that adorns it from every direction, no longer needing any independent being or state of awareness. You are there for as long as the earth itself has existed, and will. Behind you, a series of clomps awaken you. It is a great and grand beast of the forest, standing tall as the trees, with antlers that seem to scratch the heavens. He sits down beside you, lying next to you, and rests with you. You realize there are others, besides you, others existing just as close to you in this infinite wilderness as this. You lazily doze off together, and fall into his great coat, feeling his breathing, which seems to be the rumble of the entire earth, forever, and you fall asleep.

Chapter3: The Little Field Mouse Learns Magic

It was a lovely, balmy summer day. The little field mouse and her friends played the whole day in the field by the pond. They played catching, hiding and ran to the bet.

Suddenly the little field mouse said to her friends, "Do you know what, now I'll conjure something for you!" The friends looked at each other in astonishment. "You can do magic?" They sat on a recumbent tree trunk and watched the little field mouse in their preparations. This curled up a small stump and spread a cloth over it. On the other hand, she put a cylinder on the cloth and covered it with another cloth.

Then she raised her paws up: "Abracadabra." And it happened ... nothing. The friends looked a little disappointed. The little field mouse pulled the cloth from the cylinder with a "Wusch" and reached in with his left hand. At the same time she reached down with her right hand, behind the tree stump. Then she jerked up both hands and held a small cuddly toy in her right hand. The friends applauded, but a little hesitantly.

"Um ..." said the little hedgehog, "Did you get the stuffed animal out of the cylinder? Or behind the tree stump, conjured up? "" Well, tell me! "The small field mouse was awakened. "Out of the cylinder, of course!" She asserted. "That looked different," confirmed the little frog. "Yes, exactly!" The little hedgehog again invaded. "Somehow, your 'magic' does not seem quite professional." The small field mouse lowered its head. "Yes, you are right. Actually, I cannot do magic. "" Shall I teach you? "Asked the little pink piggy.

"You want to teach me magic?" Wondered the little field mouse. "Can you do that anyway?" "Klaro!" Came in response and a surprised murmur made the rounds among friends. "Show us!" Demanded the little hedgehog, who could not believe that. And the little piglet exchanged the position with the little field mouse. "Ladies and Gentlemen," it began, "now watch the famous and infamous magic show of the little pink pig!" Behavioral clapping began. The friends were not sure yet what to expect now.

"First," the magician continued, "I'll let this cuddly toy" the cuddly toy was shaken in the hand, "disappear in the cylinder!" Until now, the show did not look so bad and the little field mouse drummed with their paws a kind of drum roll on the tree trunk. The little pink piggy put the stuffed animal in the cylinder and covered it with the cloth. "Hocus and pox, the cuddly toy now disappears, but not only to the locus, but in every sense of the wind!" It waved mystically with his arms over the cylinder and pulled the cloth abruptly aside. "Ta-Taaaa!" Shouted it, putting itself in victory pose.

"Huh?" The little hedgehog let out. "The cuddly toy is still in the cylinder." "Nonsense, is not it!" Replied the pig and lifted the cylinder up and turned it around loosely Gaaaanz. When the cuddly toy should have fallen out, it did not happen. The friends got big eyes. "Where is it?" Wondered the little frog and hopped forward and examined the cylinder. In the cylinder was no cuddly toy. And there was no one behind the tree stump and the piggy had obviously no cuddly toy with him. "Hey!" Cried the little hedgehog, "you can actually do magic!" "I say!" Insisted the little pink pig.

"Then you can really teach me?" Asked the little field mouse. "Klaro!" But before that the magic show continued. "Ladies and gentlemen! Watch me spell out the cuddly toy again! "The small field mouse again made its drum roll on the tree trunk. The little frog looked at the piggy with big eyes. There's a catch, he thought, the pig CAN NOT conjure. "Aboro co Diboro! Singa Pur and Qudra Tur! Cuddly toy now come out, preferably here and not in the moor. "And again, the little piggy wagged over the cylinder with the cloth on it."TA-TAAAA!" Cried it, tore its arms up again and made the winning pose.

The clapping was a bit louder now, but stopped quickly. "I do not see it yet," the little frog grumbled again. "Should that be in the cylinder now, or what?" "Ladies and gentlemen, I'm going to turn this cylinder around slowly now." And the piggy turned the cylinder gaaaanz loosely as before. And again no cuddly toy fell out. "The cuddly toy is NOT in the cylinder. Where can it be? I've conjured it up again. "" Come on, you bang bag, tell me! "Cried the frog, who still thought it all a big scam. "My dear frog, please turn around once," said the little pink piggy.

The frog turned and saw the cuddly toy sitting on its feet behind the tree trunk on which they sat. It seemed to be smirking at the little frog. He took the cuddly toy amazed and held it up for everyone to see. And again, the pig called, "TA-TAAAAAAA!" But now the friends were clapping wildly and loud and loud. "Bravo!" "Great!" "Great!" Shouted the three spectators and the little frog patted the piggy's shoulder. "You can REALLY conjure!" And the little hedgehog rejoiced: "I know a magician! I know a magician!"

In the next few days, the little field mouse learned magic from the little pink piggy. It was not easy. It took a lot of effort to get the difficult exercises done. Some magic tricks went pretty easy. But others were really hard to learn. After a few days, she showed her friends some tricks. The friends were really excited about how well she had learned magic. They clapped, cheered and shouted for an encore. At the encore, the little pink piggy had to help out a bit. But that was the best magic show the friends had ever seen and organized.

Chapter4: The Hot Air Balloon

You feel the excitement and nervousness in your restless body as you approach the gigantic balloon. Climbing into the wicker basket, you feel your heart flutter and your stomach does a small flip. You can smell the propane and hear the burning flame ready to power this balloon into the air. Holding onto the edge of the basket you wait for your secure ascent into the air. Feeling the smooth wood beneath your hand, the drift of the slightest amount of heat from the balloon, the distant smell of a salty ocean. As the basket starts to rise you feel how tense and achy your muscles are. You concentrate on grounding yourself as your body is being lifted to unknown heights.

Digging your toes down into the floor of the basket. Feeling you're strong, sturdy ankles supporting you letting you know they won't waver, they will keep you steady. Your legs feel alive as the muscles reflectively tense and relax as you ground yourself. As you rise even higher you feel a shift in your body. The fear of the flight is leaving you, and instead, you feel an uplifting grace and peaceful presence. Your body doesn't feel as heavy as it did moments ago. The almost weightlessness you experience settles you. As you look around at the beautiful scenery you continue to stabilize your body. Relaxing your aching back, allowing the curves to blend into themselves. Your stomach settling down as you focus your thoughts on your breathing. Breathing in and expanding your lungs, delivering oxygen to your body. Breathing out, allowing your muscles to relax and await their next oxygen delivery. As you breathe in and out slowly, you can relax your shoulders, neck, and finally your mind.

As you continue relaxing and breathing, you can focus on the land growing smaller beneath you. Like the troubles, you leave behind when you sleep. The balloon drifts peacefully, you can see the ocean now. The water deeply blue, the beach over-crowded as people are eager to find the blissful relaxation that you're already able to experience. The red and white umbrellas line the crowded beach, people lying on their towels on the warm sand. You're above the beach now and people point and you can hear them hoot and holler as you soar above. Hearing the ocean lull beneath the sound of the crowd. You wave hello with a warm smile, thankful you can easily slip away from this crowded area and into your cocoon of happiness and warmth. The balloon drifts further from the crowd and noises. The ocean shrinking and becoming distant. You can no longer smell or hear the bustle that was on the ocean shore. Now, your mind is welcoming the quiet uninhabited lands you are approaching. Your nose is eager for the clean crisp scents of the fields beneath you.

Seeing many colors of wildflowers blur together as you soar above. Like a bird in a lengthy flight for winter, you take in all your surroundings. Relaxing, breathing, just being. Traveling away for your long, peaceful rest. Stepping away from the cold harshness that can sometimes be a reality, and traveling to the warm, sunny peace deep inside your mind. Below you see a laundry line and a small farmhouse; seeing the clothing dance on the line as you gently pass by as if now they are waving to you as you waved to the beachgoers. The land turns from flat and uninhabited to small rolling hills with the occasional house.

You see the town grows as you travel towards the center, more roads, more houses, and more businesses. As the path of your life; you start out fresh, not knowing many things, being able to see and know everything around you like the small farmhouse. As you age, the roads you travel become familiar, but longer, more complicated, twists and turns, connecting to other roads. The houses keep popping up as you meet new people. The businesses are opportunities that you may latch onto or let them pass by; whichever is right for you at that time in your life. The connections throughout this town or city, working like your mind often do. Growing together, supporting a singular body.

You pass over neighborhoods, seeing the quiet towns below. Friendly neighbors having cookouts and children playing kickball together. The towns pass by so quickly and it reminds you of how quickly time can seem to pass. Your mind tries to distract you, remind you of the things you need to accomplish. The things you need to worry about. It's time to quiet those thoughts. You are creating your own wind as you soar through the sky, whisper your concerns to the wind. Let them travel through the air, fall to the ground. You can pick them up at another time. Whisper the thoughts of what you need to do tomorrow. Whisper the thoughts of what you should be worrying about. Whisper anything that is on your mind. Watch the words leave your mouth, drift through your wind, fall to the ground. The words jumbling together as they spiral to the ground. Falling and falling until you can no longer see them. Those thoughts are gone now; you have freed your mind and have total control over your body.

Breathing in allowing your body to soak in the peace with a clear mind. Breathing out feeling your body sigh with relief. The hot air balloon is now traveling over the forest. The tops of the trees are green and lush. You feel like a cloud floating above the trees. The coverage dense in some areas, shielding you from the world below. While in other areas it thins out, allowing you to peek at the wonder Mother Nature has set before you.

A group of birds' flocks beside you, you can hear them calling out to each other at the curiosity you are presenting to them in this huge balloon. How odd it must be for them. You look up and are again amazed at how a little bit of heat and this huge material are allowing you to soar with birds. The rainbow color panels seem to glow as the sun shines down through them. The red panel making you think of love and warmth. The orange panel reminding you of tropical colors on an island, the flowers, the clothes, the fruits, and the peaceful setting sun. The yellow panel reminding you of pure happiness and joy; like a full warm sun, or the tart bite of a lemon. The green panel showing the reflection of life; of mother nature as it surrounds you...the green of the trees, the grass, the fields below. The blue panel, reflecting on the open clear skies. Open like your mind, absorbing the welcoming warmth of the other colors. The purple panel, reflecting its vibrant color that can be rarer than the others and is often a sign of nobility. Reflecting the rare peace and calm of complete bliss, reflecting this journey in this hot air balloon.

The forest is thinning out and you can see a beach in the distance. As you approach it you find yourself approaching a barely sandy and rocky shore, the water angrily lapping at the shoreline. While not friendly for a relaxing day at the beach, the sounds of the crashing waves reflect that of your beating heart. It's as if you can feel those waves beating against the rocks from deep within your soul. You feel the blood pumping through your body, then beating through your heart. The waves rolling in and out like your breath. Working together to create a beautiful rhythm that is essential for your life. The sounds of the ocean start to drift off until you only feel your heart, mirroring what you know the ocean is doing even in your absence.

You approach an open field, you know your journey must be near its end. As the balloon starts to descend, you feel yourself falling slightly more horizontal. Peacefully drifting into the proper place of relaxation. Your body shifts, finding the most comforting position as you feel the weight returning to your body. The heaviness weighing your body down until it feels impossible to do nothing but let it pull you down. Relax into the weight. Feel your body sinking into the warmth of the descent. Allow your tired legs to rest, pulling the rest of your body down with them. Breathe in and out slowly as you drift down into peace, lying your head back and feeling gravity welcome you home. The warmth of the balloon envelopes you as you caress the ground. The balloon is at rest. Lie here as long as you like. Rest, breath in the field around you. What does this field look like up closely? Is it fragrant flowers? Warm and mellow wheat? Close your eyes and rest for a moment. Allow your body to sink in and enjoy this complete relaxation this trip has brought you. Reflect on the sights that you have seen, only one thing stirs you from your revelry... The pilot asks you, "Do you want to go up again?"

Chapter5: The Tranquil Submarine

You feel the breeze on your face, cool as is blows over the surreal blue ocean surrounding you. You are on your way to explore the magical world of the ocean by submarine. The excitement is coursing through your body, holding your muscles stiff. You have arrived at the submarine, you stand in line, awaiting to walk the stairs down through the porthole. It is finally your turn, as you descend the stairs you come into the submersible and feel your nerves ramp up a notch as your surroundings close in. Going from the vast ocean openness around you, down into a small vessel makes your body feel even tenser. You see the many windows lining the craft, with comfortable seating in front of each.

You eagerly make your way to your seat and sit down, allowing the plush comfort to cradle your body. Your body feels fidgety and antsy as you try to sink into the comfort, let's try to calm your nerves before this journey. Inhale deeply, allowing the oxygen to reach every organ in your body. Slowly exhale, relaxing the organs as they patiently await the next inhale. As people settle in around you, ignore them, focus only on yourself. Focus on this remarkable journey you're about to experience, seeing a new side of this precious gift of life from below the water's surface. Inhale in, allowing the cool breeze of your breath travel through your body, down to toes and in between, caressing your feet, allowing them to relax as the breath warms and travels back, ready to be exhaled. Inhale again, this time focusing on the breath to travel down to your hands, in between your fingers, caressing your palms, as the breath warms and travels back to be exhaled. Inhale deeply, allowing the breath to settle your stomach, warming as it caresses your lungs, travels between your shoulder blades and back to exhale. Inhale deeply once more as the breath caresses your brain, warms it, comforts it, and then back to exhale.

You feel calm and relaxed as the pilot comes across the speaker to prepare you for the descent. He tells you to pay close attention to the right side of the vessel as the submarine descends. You turn and see a family of sea lions. A slight shift in pressure reminds you that your body is snug inside this vessel, but let it be a snugness of comfort. The friendly and curious beings approach the vessel, delighting in the bubbles as you descend. Count to see how many sea lions there are. One, two, three, four, five, six, seven; there are seven playful sea lions. They swim quickly around the submarine. One swims up to your window, looking at you as you look at it. Its curious deep brown eyes filled with wonder and excitement, reflecting the wonder in your own. As the submarine continues to descend down the creatures lose interest and swim back to where they were.

Staring out into the vast blueness of the ocean, you reflect on how hectic your life has become. How simple these creatures have it, just exist. Go through every day seeing the beauty in the world, living in it, enjoying it. You start to see small schools of fish, the pilot informs you of some of the species, but you drown out his talking and let it become a soft, lulling murmur in the background. You see fish that are bright blue with yellow tails. They dart this way and that way, minding their own business as the vessel passes them by. You see silverfish, some with stripes, some streamlined for speed, some with large graceful fins and a touch of color, traveling in the safety of numbers. All your thoughts from the day are clustered in packs like the fish in this ocean. A small shark soars by, some scatter away, some stick together and ignore the danger. Let's put those thoughts away, just let it be you here, nothing to distract your mind. Visualize the thoughts, now wrap them in a bubble and send them to the surface. They will be there for you on the surface, when you're ready for them. Each and every thought should be sent away in a bubble, watch the bubbles drift to the surface as you keep descending. Let them move further away from you, from your mind, until your mind is clear.

The pilot announces that we are off the coast of an island with lots of unusual creatures, you look closely out your window and see a lizard swim by. Unusual indeed. The pilot tells you that these are marine iguanas and they are only in this area of the world. The small monster with deep green skin, with hints or red and orange, it is beautiful as it swims down onto the vivid green moss-covered rocks. You see a few more as you travel along. Some resting on the colorful rocks, some chasing food, some swimming peacefully. The water is so clear and exquisite, it's like being in the world's largest aquarium from the inside. Seeing these creatures in their natural environment, seeing the wonder of their magnificent world is awe-inspiring. You pass through a school of many slender fish, it seems there is more fish than water at this point. The fish are so thick the submarine gets briefly dark, it's just thousands and thousands of the narrow-bodied fish outside the windows. Through the thickness, you see a bird glide through the water to snatch some of the fish for an easy meal. It is a penguin. Here in this tropical water, you see a penguin. You listen back in for the pilot to explain that these penguins are also indigenous to these islands. Who would have thought of all these wonderful creatures existing in this one magical place? You see another penguin dive down, do a spin, and then dart back up. Its body streamlined for this job of hunting these particular fish.

You realize your body has become tense again as you've moved closer and closer to the window, afraid you will miss something. Sit back, relax, focus on your breathing and just enjoy what you can see. You will not miss anything. Out your window you can see a stingray, almost black in color with white dots all over. The stingray gently lifts its wings revealing its white underside as it glides away from the vessel. As you move deeper away from the bright corals and rock and fish you notice the ocean is more open. Cold, and dark. You take the blanket off your chair and pull it snug around you. Blocking out the cold, but welcoming the dark as the low lights on the submarine flick-on. The fish are more solitary now, hesitant of the vessel instead of curious. You see a large shark pass by, ignoring the submarine... The shark drifts by in its daily routine. There will be no more descending the pilot announces and you're grateful. You feel deep in the ocean, but the peace and quiet you're experiencing is unlike any other.

Out your window you see a sunken ship. It looks old, lonely, and desolate. But it is now also a haven for many fish away from the coral. You see smaller fish darting around the ship. The local life taking over what was once a part of your world. There is an odd sensation of peace, knowing that you are in their territory, these sharks, these fish, and this deep, desolate ocean. This is their home, you are only here to visit, and they don't seem to mind. Some notice you, some don't even bother, they just let you admire. Admire how something old, tired, and broken can become something new and beautiful. This shipwreck is beautiful; harboring so much life around it. The lights illuminate how this ship belongs here now. These animals rely on its existence. This mistake that caused this ship to sink, was crucial to the survival of these animals here now. Everything is connected, everything happens for some reason. You may not always understand, but all you can do is relax and control how you feel. How your mind handles the things around you. You can have a peaceful and meaningful existence. Like this ship or like the animals around it. You have a purpose, and you will reach that purpose because that is life. The submarine travels on, leaving the ship behind.

As you leave everything behind your mind feels tired, the coldness of the ocean tries to sink through the walls of the vessel, but the cold doesn't touch you; the blanket is a warm comfort around you. You lie your head back and see through the top glass of the submarine. As your neck relaxes, like the rest of your body, you breathe slowly as a huge sea turtle gracefully glides over the submarine. You can barely see the surface anymore, the dappled sunlight dancing faintly in the dark blue water. The turtle has a dark silhouette, the occasional fish, big and small swimming above. Your body feels heavy, but relaxed. Your mind moving slow and peaceful as you take in the surroundings of the deep, vast ocean. Close your eyes as you memorize the surroundings to hold with you forever. You will always recall this peace during times of stress, you will be able to close your eyes, seeing the ocean's surface way above you as the creatures' drift peacefully overhead.

Chapter6: Marcia Wants To Live Until She Dies

I am dying. Probably not today or tomorrow, but the hard truth is I am dying. My oncologist told me I might even live for six more months, but doctors stretch the time when speaking to patients about death, so I probably have a month or two less. The test results after the second round of chemotherapy just came back. The treatment didn't stop cancer's progress.

My husband, Ben, held my hand tightly as we heard the news. I don't think either of us took a full breath until we found our way out of that office and into our car. And then we cried.

"We have to get another opinion," he said. "There must be something else we can do."

"No, Ben," I said, with a sad strength that surprised me. "I don't want to. Medicine doesn't have the answer. We both know that. Besides, don't want any more poison dripping into my veins or aseptic

Hospital rooms, and please, God, no procedures of last resort. I want to be home with you and Dorothy. I want to live until I die. Please, let's just go home." "All right, honey. Let's go home to our baby," he said sadly. "We'll talk about it later."

We drove in silence, our minds going their separate ways, our hands tightly interwoven. My tears could have filled a riverbed.

It was unfathomable to me that I was leaving my two-year-old daughter. How could it be? It didn't make sense. Just the idea was more than I could bear, which is probably why it kept slipping away, only to return a moment later with another stab of pain. All this upset must have put me in a state of shock, because the next thing I knew the scene outside the car window turned very still, silent, and exceptionally clear. The hum of the car's motor filled my ears, and the blue of the sky astounded me. Against that background, a hawk circled slowly, silently, gliding ever upward on a current of air. For a brief moment, I was that lone bird, held by the great wind, immersed in the wondrous beauty of it all. From somewhere deep inside my body came an overwhelming yearning to hold my baby, which drew me back to the earth. Strange to say, I felt not just sadness on the return but also some kind of aching joy. The moment passed quickly, and I was left wondering why the image appeared. What did it have to do with my death?

That's when I swore to live my dying as fully as possible, squeezing the very last drop of juice out of life. I would live until I died, and maybe dying would become a spiritual path. But what did that mean?

Glancing toward Ben as he made a smooth turn onto the highway that would take us home, I became aware of his tall, athletic frame and the perfection of his clear cut profile. What would this do to him? He was such a capable man, so able to make things happen. But could he manage to lose me? Would he fall apart?

Or would he find someone else? It wouldn't be long before another woman would catch sight of the easy informality of him, the shock of black hair that wouldn't quite stay in place, the shy glance when he was caught unaware. When an image of

Ben and another woman embracing came into my mind. I let out a cry.

Soon we were home, and Dorothy was in my arms. Touching her sweet soft skin, it came to me that I didn't have to find that spiritual path.

Living my life fully in the awareness of death was the path. It led us to live in the moment.

In a sense, even Dorothy's home birth had taken place on the path.

We weren't then quite as aware of death as we were now, but we were in the moment. Ben and I did it together. With a midwife presiding, there weren't any white gowns, blank walls, face masks, or mind-numbing drugs to suppress this most sacred of acts. It was just Ben and me, and the midwife. I wish you could have seen the way we all worked together to open the way for Dorothy.

Ben was best of all. Sitting on the bed right next to my head, he sensed the contractions rise, peak, and subside and breathed through them with me. When they got serious, he held my shoulders, and we rode those contractions for all they were worth. He even found ways to make me laugh when I needed some humor to manage the pain. We cried together when we saw the first patch of baby hair reflected in a well-placed mirror, and what a sense of glory when, after a few momentous pushes, Dorothy's head, her chin, and then her shoulders emerged.

Truly, Ben and I gave birth to Dorothy.

Fortunately, we were able to take off six whole weeks in maternity/ paternity leave to tend to her. At first, it was as if all three of us were inside some big womb. Ben and I spent long hours lying in bed, the baby between us, our sleep schedule merging with hers so that the difference between day and night was almost lost. It was dreamlike to be immersed in all those bodily fluids—sweet breast milk intermingling with the sweat of our bodies. Ben called it baby bliss. In the blink of an eye, however, that entire experience was gone. The tiny little infant was just a memory.

In another blink of the eye, Dorothy was one year old, sitting in her high chair in the midst of grandparents and friends.

A year later, on a table right next to me, sat a picture of that birthday scene. Ben looked particularly appealing in his black sweater and jeans.

I was the image of health, tall, lean, with long, thick red hair hanging loose down my back and a happy smile on my face. Ever mindful that my large breasts did not attract too much attention,

I was wearing one of my loose tops. Not only one year had gone, so had that attractive young woman.

The day after that party, I discovered a very small lump in the lower left quadrant of my right breast. There had been other lumps in the past, so I didn't feel like a foolish optimist concluding it probably was a cyst.

Besides, I took care of myself. I was a vegetarian and had a daily exercise routine. Ben often joked, "Marcia is our in-house nutrition consultant."

Nevertheless, I called my gynecologist, got the necessary tests, and went in to have a biopsy. A few days later, I was back sitting in her office, expecting to hear that it was nothing. Instead, she told me this time it was for real. It wasn't just a cyst. I had cancer of a rare and rapidly growing type, and it had already spread to my lymph nodes. How ironic, with all my healthy living, and my conscious avoidance of caffeine, sweets, and saturated fats, that I should be the one to have breast cancer. I could have eaten tons of junk food for all it mattered!

The only other memory I have of those early days before I started my journal, was sitting in bed late one night, with my tears and my worries tumbling out: "I'm scared, Ben. This might be terrible. It might even mean my death."

"I know you're worried. I am, too," Ben offered. "But there's good medical care out there these days. We'll find a way to get you well, Marcia.

We have to."

"I'm afraid I'll need you too much. I don't want you to feel trapped by an invalid. Besides, life is as hectic as it is. How are we ever going to manage my cancer, your job, and Dorothy?"

God, I love that man! How did I ever get so lucky as to find him?

I don't need to tell yet another cancer treatment story; by this time, you know about chemotherapy and its side effects. But I do want to describe how Ben and I worked together because I'm proud of it. Our first decision was to give ourselves the reward of a fabulous vacation in

Italy after the treatment was over. Tuscany was our place of choice. Ben brought home some travel books and even began cooking in the style of the region.

We also learned about cancer together. My oncologist, Dr. Anita Greenfield, clued me in on Websites I could use to do research, and I made use of my medical friends to network with people who had the information we needed. No way would we let the medical establishment deprive us of decision making.

But that was not all. I couldn't shake the fear that my body wouldn't be able to manage the chemo, and that Ben wouldn't be able to put up with me. So I found a therapist. She helped me understand that these discouraging thoughts were simply my worries and that I also had positive, even brave thoughts as well. And they were just as important. For instance, most of the time,

I really did think I had the strength to get through the treatment and that cancer would let go of me. I began to call those thoughts my convictions. Then I learned how to practice replacing my worries with my convictions. It helped.

Finally, the wonder of wonders, the chemotherapy, and the six weeks of radiation was actually over. I had another round of life, blessed life. It's impossible to fully tell you how much the morning light meant to me. The symphony of the crickets, the whoosh of the wind, Dorothy's giggle when we played peek-a-boo—all the small things that made my heart soar.

The three of us went out to dinner that night. Ben and I drank champagne.

Dorothy had her apple juice.

Life went back to normal, not pre-cancer normal but something that might be called post-cancer extraordinary-normal. Sure there was work and play and all the worry about any small ache in my body. But we also took that trip to Italy.

Three glorious weeks! We rented what was once a small farmhouse not too far from Florence, and Dorothy marched her way through town after town, her gleeful face attracting more attention than we ever thought possible. Grown men stopped in the middle of the street to play with her; mothers asked if she could have a piece of candy. With Dorothy around, we didn't need to know how to speak Italian. Parents have a universal language.

My senses were wide open. I remember waking up to the cool fresh air coming through our bedroom window and the sounds of birds, chickens, and an occasional person tending the supports in the vineyard down in the valley below. Ben and I fell in love again during those early mornings before Dorothy got up. It was a new kind of love, a post-cancer extraordinary-love we would say to each other, as we learned our bodies all over again. Never before had we paid such close attention to the simple feeling of being hugged. I relished being encircled in his arms with my head tucked into his neck, our bodies touching down the whole length of me. He delighted in resting his head on my breast, with my arms holding him fully, tightly. When Dorothy woke up and came toddling into the room for a few precious moments, she settled in between us in still another kind of hug.

Chapter7: A Snowman Saves Christmas

Once upon a time there was a snowman who lived in the Christmas wonderland high on a hill in a house sitting on a tree. It was not a tree house. It was a real house in a tree. It was normal in the Christmas Wonderland. There were also gingerbread houses, huge Christmas trees and much more fantastic.

But let's get back to our snowman, whose biggest wish was to be a Christmas elf. However, only elves were allowed to be Christmas Elves. It was written in the big Christmas book.

Nevertheless, the snowman tried it year after year. He disguised himself once as an elf to get into the magnificent Christmas factory. But he already noticed the guard on the gate. Maybe his carrot had betrayed him on the face? Or maybe he was just more spherical than anyone else.

It will work this year. Because the snowman had a great idea. He wanted to pack presents himself and distribute them to the children. But could Santa not be angry with him? And he could finally conjure the longed-for smile into the faces of the children.

First, the gifts had to come from. But where to take and not steal? He had to make some money somehow. But what should he do? He sled incredibly well on the sled. But you could not earn money with that.

He remembered something. He slid happily and started to make little snowballs. Then he took a sign and sat down in the snow. On the sign it was written: "Every Ball 3 Taler". That would have to work. Everyone likes snowball fights. But the snowman was sitting in vain hour after hour. Nobody even bought a snowball.

So he asked the blacksmith if he could help. He only laughed loudly. "What do you want to help me with?" The blacksmith asked. "If you stand by the fire with me, you'll melt. Do you want to serve me as drinking water? "

"That's right." Thought the snowman. It had to be something cold. So he went to the ice factory. There large blocks of ice were made to build igloos. But even here, the snowman was laughed at. "How do you want to help me?" Asked the factory manager. "The blocks are so heavy, if you want to push them, break your thin stick sleeves."

"That's right." Thought the snowman again. It has to be something where it's cold and the work is not too hard. So the snowman went to the ice cream seller. He was taken with the idea and said: "You are certainly a good ice cream seller! You're never too cold, and if ice is missing for cooling, we'll just take something from you. "

When the snowman heard that, he was startled. "Ice cream from me?" He asked. "I think I was wrong in the door," he said and walked quickly away.

Now the snowman was sad. Nothing he tried worked. He sank to the ground in the middle of the city. His hat slipped over his sad button eyes. He picked up his violin and played a Christmas carol. That always helped him when he was sad.

As he played, he was so lost in thought that he did not notice the passing people throwing him some change. Only when a stranger passed in said: "A wonderful Christmas carol. That's one of my favorites. Keep playing snowman. "He listened.

He pushed his hat up and saw the change in front of him. "That's money!" He said softly. And played on. "That's money!" He shouted loudly and kept playing. He grinned all over his face and sang with his heart's content: "Tomorrow children will give something. Tomorrow we will be happy ..."

With the newly earned money, he bought gifts and wrapping paper. A doll there and a car here. Hardworking was packed and laced. And the cord passed through the hole. "One right, one left - yes the snowman comes and brings it!"

But wait. How should the presents reach the children from here? The snowman considered. "I cannot wear it. But I do not have a Christmas sleigh either. And Santa will hardly lend me his. Besides, the reindeer would want to eat my carrot. "

The snowman could sled incredibly well on a sledge, but it was not always just mountain off. So what to do? Again, the snowman had a great idea. He tied the presents to a snail. Snails can carry a lot. That would work.

Just when he was done, a Christmas elf passed by. "What will that be when it's done?" The Christmas elf asked. The snowman stood proudly next to his snail. "This is my Christmas slug! And I'm giving presents to the children this year. "

The Christmas elf looked at the snowman and the snail in wonderment. "I would laugh now, if it were not so sad," he said then. "You know that a snail is way too slow to deliver gifts to all the children in the world? I mean, she herself would be too slow to supply just this village. "

The happy grin passed by the snowman and the elf continued: "In addition, unfortunately, these are not enough gifts. You would need a million billion more. But it does not matter anyway. Anyway, Christmas is out this year! "

When the snowman heard that, he no longer understood the world. "Christmas is out? That does not work! "The Christmas elf nodded:" And if that works. Santa Claus got sick and cannot distribute presents. "

"Naaaein", the snowman breathed in astonishment and looked at the elf in disbelief. "Santa Claus cannot get sick." The Christmas elf nodded again: "That's right. Usually not. But this year it's so cold that even our Christmas elves are too cold. "The snowman got nervous:" But Christmas, so Christmas ... so, what about Christmas? "He ran around hectic and talked to himself:" No, no, no, no, that cannot be. A Christmas without presents is not a Christmas. "

The Christmas elf interrupted the snowman. "Christmas is very Christmas without gifts. The presents were getting more and more and almost too much over the last few years anyway. "The snowman collapsed briefly and breathed out," Yeah, yaaaaaaaaaa, that's alright. "Then he stood straight up and said," But with presents it's a lot more beautiful."

The Christmas elf shook his head: "Christmas is the festival of charity. No need for presents. "The snowman whirled around and said quietly," Yes, that's right. "Then he took one of his presents and held it up to the Christmas elf's nose." But look how beautiful the presents are. With such a gift, I can show my charity much better than without. "

Then he let the gift disappear behind his back and looked at the Christmas elf sadly. "Look, now it's gone. Is not that sad? Imagine the many little sad googly eyes standing in front of a Christmas tree, under which there are no presents. And now tell the children that we do not need presents, because Christmas is the feast of charity! "

The Christmas elf said, "Okay, maybe you're right. But what should we do? It's too cold! "The snowman tossed the gift aside and slid to the Christmas elf:" Ha! Exactly! It's too cold! ... For Santa Claus. But I'm a snowman! "Then he turned in a circle and began to sing:" I'm never too cold, I'll be so old. I can hurry and hurry, distribute gifts to children. All you have to do is help me with stuff and team. Take me to Santa Claus quickly. "

The Christmas elf covered its ears: "Now stop singing. I'll take you there already. "The snowman jumped in the air with joy:" Juhu! Hey, that was almost rhyming. You could also sing a song. "And so the snowman talked a long while on the way to Santa - to the chagrin of the Christmas Elf.

Arriving at Santa Claus, he was very surprised to see a snowman at home. Usually there were only Christmas elves. But Santa Claus loved the idea that Christmas should not be canceled. Because he was of the opinion that Christmas is simply nicer with gifts. But how should the snowman distribute so many presents?

The snowman chewed nervously on his lips. He was so close to living his biggest dream. "We do not have to distribute all presents," he said. "Everyone gets a little less this year. It's still better than nothing, isn't it? "Santa looked at the snowman:" I do not think that's a bad idea. That should work! But how do you want to drive the presents? You cannot have my sled! "

The snowman was on the verge of despair. "Only solve this one problem and my dream comes true." He thought. Then he said sheepishly, "Well, I'm a pretty good sledger!" And looked questioningly at Santa. The Christmas elf intervened: "Oh, that's all nonsense! Then you only supply the children who live at the bottom of a mountain? Or how should I imagine that? "

But Santa raised his hand and moved his fingers as if he were scratching the air. Out of nowhere a huge snow slide emerged under the snowman. Then Santa said, "You're such a good sledger. This snow mountain will accompany you. He is a never ending snow slope. So you can go sledding anywhere. "

The snowman looked at the huge snow mountain and said: "That .... Is ... "he suddenly jumped in the air and shouted loudly:" ... the hammer! Sledding! That's not what I imagined in my wildest dreams. "

The snowman was happy as never before. But Santa raised his index finger again and said admonishingly: "But watch out by the fireplaces! I've burnt my butt once before! "But the snowman let it go cold:" Oh, I have so much snow, if I burn my butt, I'll just make a new one - haha. "Then he grinned at Santa, jumped on his sled and was gone.

And so the snowman saved Christmas, which was way too cold, but just right for the snowman!

Chapter8: Gaia's Great Dance

Once upon a time, there was a magical, mystical figure that grew out of the earth; actually, she really was of the earth, and she was called Gaia. Gaia was the most beautiful female figure you could ever imagine, and you could imagine whatever you wanted because she would become that for you. Her biggest job, each year, was to come out of the earth and wake up the land in time for spring. She got to sleep throughout the long winter while her counterpart Boreas was playing with his magic. When springtime comes, it is Gaia's turn to frolic throughout the land. Her magic was quite different from the magic released during winter. While all seasons have equal importance for some reason or the other, spring is truly the most important for the continuing cycle of life. Once the earth and the plants and the animals have rested, it is time for them to revive and to renew. Without Gaia, we would have no food or air, no life or love. She must awake and dance to her peculiar music, luring the plants to peek out of the ground and coaxing the animals to bring forth new babies.

Her winter blanket of snow and ice starts to melt, and the ground in which she sleeps starts to thaw. Every time she stretches her arms and yawns, a new branch appears on a tree or a bud springs out of the ground. Because she has been sleeping for so long now, several months, it takes her a while to wake up. But you can tell when that awakening begins because little things start to happen all around you.

Slowly and steadily, the world starts to fill with small sounds that are absent during the winter. Instead of the thick, quiet sound of falling snow, you will start to hear the pitter-pat of gentle rain drops announcing that spring is very much on its way. Gaia has come out of her earthly bed and started her annual dance. She first washes the dirty grey snow and brown earth off of her, causing the sweet rain showers of early spring. The ground drinks this thirstily, preparing for all of the new life that will soon be bursting from it. Instead of the dark, silent mornings of winter, you will start to hear the slight chirping of birds, as Gaia waves her arms through the air, welcoming the flocks back from the winter vacation. The slight chirpings through your window will be accompanied by a brighter and brighter sliver of sunlight as the season grows stronger and Gaia smiles broader. You might start to hear the soft breeze of springtime start to blow through branches that are slowly awakening along with everything else. After the stillness of winter, the world starts to feel electric with energy, awakening slowly but surely, as it does every year.

You will also start to see the effects of Gaia's great dance: each time she stomps her feet, a new bud pops out of the ground. Each time she waves her arms, a new green leaf appears on a tree. Her rhythmic, elegant dance gives each and every living thing a new reason to be, a new season to grow. First, you will start to see the tender herbs of mint and chives growing up from the ground. Then, you start to see heartier plants and trees putting out their new leaves and stems and flowers. In the wintertime, it only appears as if everything is gone, but really, nature is just resting, waiting for Gaia's energetic dance to bring it back to live. The bright tulips stick their heads out, brightening the world day by day by day, as Gaia continues her dance into spring.

The greening of the world continues as she twirls about, picking up the first fresh daisies of spring and ringing them round her beautiful hair like a crown. She looks like the most beautiful faerie that you've ever seen, and she is so large that she brings this new life everywhere. You can only catch glimpses of her out of the corner of your eye, but you can see her handiwork everywhere. The grass begins to grow tall and sweet again, making food for the animals to eat. The trees branch out taller and broader, with new green leaves for the insects to eat. And the insects provide food for the chirping birds that come back to nest in the spring. Gaia works her special magic, weaving her hair into braids so she can dance with ever more freedom.

She dips her toe into the chilly water of the lake and stream, warming it instantly with her great energy and joy. She must bathe herself each day, and in doing so, she infuses the water with new life. Small schools of fish tickle her bare toes, while others dart in and out of her hair, combing the great long strands into glowing health. The once frozen waters, stuck and without motion, start to flow again, bringing fresh spring water to the earth and to the plants and to the animals. The water flows throughout the land, showing how everything is connected: the land needs warm water to help the plants grow, while the animals need the plants for food. Gaia's spring is the best time of year to notice how everything in our environment works together and needs one another.

Spring represents the deepest connections between all living things: without the warmth of the sun and the green of the earth, we wouldn't have food to eat and air to breathe. Gaia welcomes all of nature's creatures to join her in her dance, and she ensures that the new crops will spring up out of the earth so that life can continue onward and new life can begin. Sometimes, when she does a particularly sprightly jig, she causes a thunderclap to explode in the sky, and if she grows weary, clouds will darken the sky while she rests for a minute. The sky will take over, filling with dark clouds and streaks of thunderbolts, bringing the drenching rains that will keep the earth watered and strong. Sometimes these storms grow scary and too strong, but Gaia renews her promise with each year, dancing just enough to wake everything up. The storms will pass, she reminds us with the twitter of the birds and the beaming of the sun, and those big showers will always bring more flowers.

It is not just the earth itself that comes back to life in the spring; it is also the sun, which grows warmer, and the animals who grow livelier. In fact, spring is the time for animals to make babies, little spring lambs and goats and rabbits: when the weather grows warmer, the baby animals grow up stronger, because they have lots of sunshine and food to eat. The babies will be born in the spring and grow up through the summer and fall, so they will be strong enough to withstand the cold of Old Man Winter and his spells. You can see baby chicks in their nests, trilling for mom to bring them a juicy worm from the damp ground. You can see baby rabbits bounding through the fields, nibbling on grass and herbs and flowers. You can see baby deer in the greening forest, bounding about on wobbly legs as the butterflies flit about, making the green world look alive from every turn. Gaia is so full of energy from her long winter sleep that she can dance through March and April and May, bringing another cycle of new, young life to fruit.

Gaia can also inspire us through her jolly dancing, as we get outside more often, to enjoy the sights and sounds and smells of the new season. While we ourselves don't have the power to awaken the land, we do have the power to coax every bit of life out of it. We can help Gaia in her annual dance by planting seeds into the ground and helping them to grow. When you plant your seeds in spring, you can harvest food and flowers in summer and fall. It is our way to help Gaia in her great and wonderful dance bring the world back to life and continue the cycle of the seasons. Not only can we plant seeds of life, but we can also plant seeds of joy: Gaia's springtime festival draws us out of our warm winter caves; we feel like running and playing and dancing in the warming sun or splashing in the warm puddles of spring rain. After a long, dark winter of being inside by the fire or in front of the screen, we take out our bicycles and roller skates, our basketballs and baseball gloves, and run along outside to celebrate the coming of spring.

Gaia is always so proud of all her accomplishments. She lifts the grey skies and brings the green plants up from out of the earth. There are festivals, too, in the spring, for everyone around the world. We celebrate the renewal of life with wonderful food and ceremonies, depending on where we are from. Each season of the year brings with it special delights, and while Boreas gets to revel in bringing people together around the hearth to celebrate the conclusion to yet another year, Gaia gets to revel in bringing people together to celebrate new beginnings. If you pay attention, you can actually see how Gaia slowly begins to awake, at the beginning of March, with tiny buds and shoots rising up from the ground. As she gains speed and energy, twirling wildly, the buds and shoots turn into great plants and flowers, while the trees bush out with endless fronds of green. By May, the world is bright and warm and full of brand new life.

After all of her daily dancing, of course, Gaia gets very sleepy, just like you do when you play outside all day long. Her body is tired from enjoying the new sun, while her mind must rest to prepare for another day. She decides she must rest each night under the light of the moon, soaking in its rays to recharge her spirit for the next wild dance of tomorrow. She gathers the moss at the edge of a vast lake to make a pillow for her weary head, and she pulls up the blanket of freshly grown grass with its soft mass and sweet smell. She yawns mightily, the last gentle breeze of a spring day, as she lays down in her earthly bed. The moon's light is pale and comforting, and the busy sounds of the spring day drift into a slow silence, as all the young creatures slumber. Gaia falls gently asleep, listening to the slowly quieting sounds of the new life that she has danced into being all around her. While she sleeps, she dreams of the next day—and the next and the next—when spring blossoms all about. The baby sheep she counts bound over her with joy.

Chapter9: Baggi's unwanted slide

Baggi loves to dig big holes. For that Baggi is still such a small excavator, he is already really fast. Once he grows up, he wants to be as big and strong a digger as his dad. They dredge huge piles of soil and debris in no time from one end of the construction site to another. The construction workers needed it for days. A strong excavator, like Baggis Papa, can do it in a few hours.

Baggi likes helping his dad with digging and so he has been to construction sites often. So often that he knows the environment like his own shovel. But that does not mean that things do not go wrong again and again.

Today, a house is to be built. For that the construction workers need a big hole in the earth. Said and done. Baggi gets going. Although he can dig really fast, he has to work hard to keep up with his daddy. Shovel by shovel, the hole grows larger quickly. Shovel after shovel but it is also fast deep. Baggi is so energetic and anxious to show his father what he is capable of, that he becomes overzealous.

He rolls faster and faster between the dug earth and the hole. It starts to drizzle. Baggis dad calls for a bad-weather break immediately - because safety first! But Baggi is at it right now and does not dream of stopping now.

But the wetter the earth gets, the slipperier it will be. Suddenly Baggi starts to skid. With momentum he rushes towards the hole. Even frightened by the unwanted slide and full of effort the little Baggi tries to slow down. But once you're in the slip, even the best brake will not help.

Baggi has an idea. He pushes his little shovel with all his strength into the ground. Now he is pulling a deep furrow and an ever-increasing pile of mud behind him. So the little Baggi tries to brake. And his plan seems to work out too, because he is getting bit by bit slower.

But unfortunately he came too late to this brilliant idea, because on the edge of the hole he is now on the loose and desperately trying to shift his weight forward so as not to slip into the huge hole.

Baggis slide was so fast that Baggis dad had not heard the fast-paced drama. Seeing Baggi on the tip, he rushes to his son's aid immediately. The wet ground does not make it easy for him. And so he comes to a tire length too late. Directly in front of him the small excavator slides straight into the hole. Behind him slips the wet earth, which he had accumulated during the slide.

Smudged and smudged with mud and earth, the little excavator now squats in the huge hole. As much as he tries to come out again, he finds no support. The wheels spin in the wet soil and he digs deeper into the earth. Even his strong dad cannot reach him now.

"Just stay calm my boy. We'll get you out of there! "Shouts Baggis dad. Then he looks up and sees the construction workers standing on the other side of the hole. They are sprinkled with mud from top to bottom. Baggi had been so eager to get out of the hole that the mud had flown in a high arc to the construction workers. These now stand like drowned poodles on the edge and wipe the muddy ground from the face.

But on the job site, fortunately, one is a big family and not at all resentful. Because especially during construction something can go wrong. The important thing is that you help each other then.

The foreman taps the dirt from the radio. Then he immediately informs the crane driver: "Excavator in need!". The crane operator sees what is going on and swings the crane over the hole to free Baggi from his predicament.

Happy to have solid ground under the wheels, Baggi is relieved. But he is also embarrassed. For one thing, he should have listened to the security regulations and thus his dad. And on the other hand, everyone will surely make fun of him and tell funny stories about him.

But to Baggis astonishment no one makes fun of him. But on the contrary. Everyone is really worried about the little excavator and asks him if everything is alright and how it happened? Baggi tells the story from the beginning. After a while, he realizes that he is telling a funny story about himself. And that is really funny! The construction workers have a lot of fun listening to Baggis story. And since it is raining right now, no more work is done today anyway. But still laughed a lot and Baggi laughs heartily with!   One bed free and one for three?

Today I tell you a story about a little girl named Lydia. Lydia is 4 years old and always nice and good. Mom and Dad are very proud that they have such a sweet child. Mum often even says "My Angel" to Lydia, because she is as good as an angel. But there is one thing that mom and dad do not find so divine. Lydia sleeps in her parents' bed every night.

How come? Surely you are asking yourself now. Does not she have her own bed? But she has. And even very cuddly. With many stuffed animals and a lot of space for such a little girl as Lydia. But Lydia just does not want to sleep in her own bed. She finds it much more comfortable with mom and dad.

At the same time, Lydia does not know what it's like to sleep in her own bed. That was so long ago that she forgot.

Mom and dad love Lydia very much. But as big as mom and daddy's bed is, it's a little tight for three. Especially since Lydia gets bigger and bigger. When the dad turns around at night, he nudges Lydia. Then Lydia awakens briefly and turns around too. She bumps into her mom and the mom is awake and turns around. And when dad turns around again, the game starts again.

Sometimes Lydia twitches in her sleep. She then dreams something and begins to fidget with her arms and legs. Lydia herself does not notice. But depending on how she's lying, either mom or dad is lucky enough to get hit. Of course one wakes up on it. And if you do not sleep enough, you are not well rested in the morning.

If Lydia wants to play during the day, mom and dad are way too broken. You did not sleep much. And it was exhausting enough to do the work and the household.

Lydia thinks that's stupid. The solution would be so simple. She would only have to sleep in her own bed. Then mom and dad would have slept well and cheerful enough to play with Lydia.

Lydia used to sleep in her own bed when she was younger. There she liked to cuddle with her teddy. But Lydia does not remember that. At some point she got a new bed - because she got bigger. And she did not sleep once in the new bed.

If Mama Lydia had asked her if she would like to sleep in her own bed, then Lydia said, "No." Lydia said more. But today Mama said something for the first time that made Lydia think. "Your teddy is certainly very sad and misses you very doll."

Lydia did not even think that when she sleeps with Mom and Dad, her stuffed animals are all alone. And indeed, her stuffed animals were already very sad. The little brown teddy, her doll, the white rabbit Mr. Schlappohr and her little pink unicorn were all alone. Of course, that had to be changed immediately.

As Mama was packing laundry in the bedroom, Lydia scurried past her. The stuffed animals in her arms. Lydia placed the cuddly toys on Mom's and Dad's bed and said, "Problem solved." Then she rubbed her hands like daddy when he finished something.

Mama did not have that in mind when she told Lydia about the sad stuffed animals. She knelt down in front of Lydia and said, "My angel. That's not OK. So we do not have enough space in the bed. We can hardly sleep that way."

Lydia thought for a moment. That's right, there was another problem. Mom and Dad were always too tired. Should she try to sleep in her own bed? Discouraged, she breathed out, "Phew. You and Dad are so far away. "She said. Mom looked at Lydia, "You mean when you sleep in your bed?" "Yes!" Lydia answered.

Now Mom thought, "Hm." Then she said, "What do you think if we leave your door a bit open. And we also leave ours a bit open. Then we'll hear you immediately, if anything should be. "

Lydia looked incredulous. But mom had an idea. "We'll try that out right away. That will be fun. What do you say? "Lydia nodded and ran to her room," Hello Mom! "She exclaimed. And mom answered, "Hello Lydia, my angel!"   It actually worked. Lydia could hear Mama without Mom having to scream. So the two spent a while and made all sorts of funny sounds that the other had to guess.

When Dad came home, he went with him immediately. Now Mama called from the bedroom, Lydia from the nursery and dad from the room. That was funny. But dad had also brought two surprises.

Once a totally cuddly blanket and a great nightlight. The blanket was pink. Because Lydia loves pink. There were also little flowers on it, which almost looked like starlets. Asterisks would have preferred Lydia, but the flowers glowed in the dark and that was great.

The nightlight actually made little stars. If you turned it on, there were little glowing stars all over the nursery. When Dad said that the night light is extra for the night and allowed to stay all night, Mama immediately said, "Well, you see. Not only can you hear us, you can see everything in your room at night."

Now Lydia liked her room a lot better. And mom also had some news. Because if Lydia slept in her own bed now, then she was already big and brave. That's why Lydia was allowed to stay awake 15 minutes longer every evening. Lydia was happy and she felt really grown up.

After supper Lydia got ready for bed. From the bathroom she marched straight into Mom's and Dad's bedroom. What was going on now? Lydia wanted to sleep in her own bed today. Oh well, the stuffed animals were still there. Well, they had to be fetched, of course.

Then Lydia cuddled up with the new blanket in her cot. Teddy, Mr. Schlappohr, her doll and her unicorn around. The great nightlight sparkled and Mama read her another story. This Lydia could fall asleep really nice. She was sound asleep. And she even dreamed of something nice.

Chapter 10: The Danish King

Denmark is high up north, where Germany stops. There is still a king there today, but he is no longer there to govern, but usually visits kindergartens because his wife likes children so much.

But a long time ago, the Danish king was very powerful. As all kings used to do, he always wanted to increase his land so that he would become even more powerful. So he also had to conquer another country. That was not easy. In the south of Denmark was Germany, then the kingdoms of Hanover and Prussia. He could not mess with them because they had many more soldiers than he. Likewise the Swedes, whose country lies next to Denmark.

So he looked north. Far behind the sea was Greenland. This is a huge country, but at the time it was very little known and it was supposed to be very cold there. So he had three ships loaded from the royal fleet. On each he put a brave knight and several soldiers, as well as horses and all kinds of war equipment.

Then it went off to Greenland in the terribly cold north. When the ships arrived, they first saw a lot of ice and snow. The knights put on their armor and went ashore to conquer it. But no one was visible and the knights froze in their iron armor on the ice, so they could not move. They kicked wildly, clawing their iron armor hard to free themselves from the ice.

A few of the other soldiers had to make a fire to get them released. As a result, of course, the armor on the feet were pretty hot and the knights burned their feet. They hopped around wildly until they were finally free and quickly disappeared on the ship.

Then one tried to bring the horses ashore, because one should conquer Greenland. The horses struggled hard, but after a few meters they also got stuck in the snow. The soldiers could not walk in the high snow and froze miserably, so that finally all went with their horses back on the ships and Greenland could not conquer first. When the knights sat around thinking and pondering, the lookout on the ship's mast reported "Enemy ahead!!"

And indeed the knights saw in astonishment how a sleigh came with very small horses. They were astonished even more when they discovered that it was not horses but many dogs in front of a sled so effortlessly whizzing across the snow.

Everyone brought their rifles and lances and feared that they would have to defend themselves. But there was only one man on the sled, an Eskimo. He greeted them in a very friendly way and was happy to see so many people, because in Greenland not so many people live and one is often quite lonely and alone. He welcomed everyone and asked them if they would not visit him in the evening, his wife would cook a nice soup of seal meat for them.

From whom you are greeted so friendly, you can fight badly against, and so put three of the knights on the dogsled, but without their heavy armor. Husch - you rushed over the landscape to a strange hut, which was made entirely of snow. It's called an igloo and it's round, but it's very nice and warm!

When they had eaten, they thanked each other and the Eskimo drove them back to their ships by dog sled. Then it was decided to drive back to Denmark.

They then reported everything to the king. He held advice with his ministers how to conquer Greenland. They also asked a wise old man named Count Johannsen. The count whispered his suggestion in the ear of the king and he was thrilled!

He sent his steward to the city to buy whatever vanilla powder he could get. Then he equipped a ship again, but this time the knights should put on thick fur coats and take sledges with them. In addition, the whole load compartment was full of vanilla powder!

Arrived in Greenland, they were greeted by Eskimos again, it was already known by now. The soldiers from Denmark brought a lot of fresh snow and made it with their vanilla powder from delicious vanilla ice cream. They gave it to the Eskimos.

They had never eaten anything like that! They were crazy about it and still wanted to have more. The knights, however, kept everything under wraps and first wanted to speak to the eskimo leader, who was quickly brought for them. With him, the knights made a contract that now Greenland would belong to Denmark and for that the Eskimos would get as much vanilla ice cream as they could eat.

Then the knights sailed home with their ship and told their king that Greenland would now belong to Denmark, without there being a war! And that's how it is today, so you can ask every Dane.

Chapter11: Moving Towards Eternal Rest

You must've died. You don't remember how, but you know it to be true. Everything dies, eventually, somewhere, and goes somewhere. Now you are here. You are walking on a cloud. All you see is light, and it is blinding, and you can make nothing out besides its own infinity, but you know that there is a giant crowd surrounding you, a crowd larger than the current population of the earth you just left, and they are all embracing you, and they are all your familiars, and they are all welcoming you to this new place. You feel guided along, and you progress with ease. This is wonderful, whatever it is. Whatever may have happened that put you here, however tragic, however painful, it is totally gone, and you are here, and it is magnificent. Even though they are invisible, the presences around you are somehow taking form in your mind, whatever your mind is, here, now that your physical body has gone. You still feel as if you are using somebody, but maybe this is just the spirit acclimating to a new form, projecting what it is familiar with as a means to cope with its new surroundings. Life on earth is its own eternity, after all, and it programs with it many things that are fleeting when eventually devoid of space and time. These invisible figures have shapes, and names, and smells, and sizes, and are their own beings, however you perceive them in this infinite void. That is your grandmother. That is your uncle. That is your friend from high school. That is someone you passed on the street and they smiled and it moved you. They are here with you, as they always have been, but closer, right next to you. It is as if you are in a singular personal embrace with every single person that has ever touched your life in a positive way, and they are all together, yet all separate, and all immediately in front of you. You are too amazed to even begin to the find the questions that you feel you should be asking, but maybe these earthly conceits are naturally falling from you, as the infinite knowledge of this form and this place begin to shut out whatever you knew previously, whatever your worldly thoughts were, and your desires, and your way of being. Those questions must have been pretty silly. This is an overpowering light that you have become a part of, were always a part of, but are just now seeing with whatever your eyes are now. Where is God? This is the question you have, unable to focus on any single individual in the infinite mass before you. But there is your answer. The reason that you can't make out the individual shapes of those beings around you is because you are seeing all that is, all there ever was, and that is God. God is all you can see now, and the infinite spectrum of life merely exists within. You are God, you are with God, and you are home. With that realization, the body ceases to be, and you are no longer on a cloud, but are in a sea of information, an electrical signal existing somehow independently yet totally a part of some vast network. The reason all these figures you had perceived were perceived as so close yet so far away is because you are now functioning beyond the speed of light. You are here, there, and everywhere. You have totally transcended the medium of physical life on earth. In a split second, you have conversations with all of your past relatives, known and unknown, and all intangibilities as they pertain to your past are reconciled. Then, before the second is over, you have conversed with all those on the periphery, those people who you had come into contact with in your previous life that came and went and were forgotten. They, too, are reconciled, all that they have to reconcile is forgotten, eternity passes by, and you are past any awareness of your previous life, going into the utmost eternal. All information is at your fingertips, yet, in this infinite stay, is rendered unexciting; it merely is. For a lifetime, you go from one side of the universe to the next, infinite sides, infinite angles, like a diamond with more surfaces that the entire population of earth could count over its entire lifespan. And once you have traversed every plane, and seen all there is to see, you become still. And in your stillness, you are still everywhere, everywhere at once, still moving faster than can be measured, but now, as well, slow; slow to the point of not even moving. You are your own plane of existence. God visits you, your family visits you, and they, too, are still, just existing besides you. Whatever you are, it will continue. An offer is given to you, to step outside of this light and into a light beyond, a light where you will cease to exist as you have ever been. Where you are now still aware of your individuality as you exist, this will stop, and you will become the whole without awareness of the self. After all you have experienced, this seems like the only option to further your own progress. As it is with all lives, you agree. The

66

stage is set, the path is made clear, and the crowd that had once welcomed you now is gathered again, intangible as ever, to see you off. Wherever they are, they are right there with you, and they are all watching you pass into the next realm. The door opens, and you are floating up into it. For the sake of its own importance, what could occur at the speed of light is now slowed down for the momentous occasion. You are slowly, slowly, slowly, floating upwards. Floating upwards towards the door. Bleeding slowly into the light beyond the light, the light that is eternal darkness. You are the door, and you transcend the door, and then you are asleep.

Chapter12:Vanka Story

Vanka Chukov, a nine-year-old boy, whom they had placed three months ago at the house of the shoemaker housing to learn the trade, did not go to bed on Christmas night.

When the masters and the officers went to the church to attend Mass of the Rooster at about twelve o'clock, he took from the closet a bottle of ink and a penholder with an enrobed pen, and, placing before him a much wrinkled sheet of paper, he prepared to write.

Before he started, he directed a look at the door that painted the fear of being surprised, looked at the dark icon in the corner, and breathed a long breath.

The paper was on a bench, before which he was on his knees.

"Dear Grandfather Constantine Makarich," he wrote, "it is I who writes to you." I congratulate you on the occasion of Christmas, and I ask God to fill you with happiness. I have no dad or mom; I only have you...

Vanka looked at the dark window, whose crystals reflected the spark plug, and imagined his grandfather Constantine Makarich, currently employed as a night guard at the house of Mr. Chivarev. He was a lean and lively old man, always smiling and with the eyes of a drinker. He was sixty-five years old. During the day, he slept in the kitchen or joked with the cooks, and at night he walked around, wrapped in a large pinch, around the farm, and occasionally struck a small square iron with a stick, to attest to He didn't sleep and scare the thieves. He was accompanied by two dogs: Cinnamon and Snake. The latter deserved his name: he was long-bodied and very clever, and always seemed to hide evil intentions; although he looked at everyone with caressing eyes, he did not inspire anyone's confidence. It was guessed,

He liked to approach people gently, without being noticed, and bite them on the calves. He frequently stole chickens from the peasants' houses. They beat him up; twice, he had been about to die hanged; but he always came out alive from the most hurried trances and was resurrected when they were already dead.

At that moment, Vanka's grandfather would be, fixedly, at the door, and looking at the illuminated windows of the church, would tease the cooks and the maids, rubbing their hands to warm up. Laughing with senile giggles would give women go.

-Do you want a powder? I would ask them, bringing the snuffbox to their nose.

The women would sneeze. The old man, rejoicing, would burst into laughter and squeeze the hands together with both hands.

Then I would offer dogs a powder. Canelo would sneeze, shake his head, and, with the sullen gesture of a man offended in his dignity, would leave. The Snake, hypocritical, always hiding his true feelings, would not sneeze and shake his tail.

The weather would be superb. There would be a great calm in the atmosphere, clear and fresh. In spite of the darkness of the night, the whole village would be seen with its white roofs, the smoke from the chimneys, the trees silvery with frost, the heaps of snow. In the sky, thousands of stars seem to make the Earth wink happy. The Milky Way would be distinguished very well, as if, on the occasion of the party, they had washed and rubbed it with snow ...

Vanka, imagining all this, sighed.

He took the pen again and continued writing:

«Yesterday they hit me. The teacher grabbed me by the hair and gave me a few straps for falling asleep, lulling his baby. The other day the teacher sent me to gut a sardine, and I, instead of starting at the head, started by the tail; Then, the teacher took the sardine and hit me in the face with her. The other apprentices, as they are older than me, mortify me, send me to the tavern vodka, and make me steal cucumbers from the teacher, who, when she finds out, shakes my dust. I am almost always hungry. In the morning, they give me a beggar of bread; to eat, some buckwheat porridge; for dinner, another bread beggar. They never give me anything else, not even a cup of tea. I sleep in the portal and spend a lot of cold; Besides, I have to lull the baby, who doesn't let me sleep with his screams ... Grandpa: Be good, get me out of here, I can't stand this life. I greet you with great respect, and I promise to always ask God for you. If you don't get me out of here, I will die.

Vanka pouted, rubbed her eyes with her fist, and couldn't suppress a sob.

"I'll be as useful as I can," he continued moments later. I will pray for you, and if you are not happy with me, you can hit me all you want. I will look for work, I will keep the flock. Grandpa: I beg you to get me out of here if you don't want me to die. I would escape and go to the village with you, but I don't have boots, and it's too cold to go barefoot. When I grow up, I will keep you with my work, and I will not let anyone offend you. And when you die, I will beg God for the rest of your soul, as I beg you now for my mother's soul.

«Moscow is a very big city. There are many palaces, many horses, but not a sheep. There are also dogs, but they are not like those in the village: they do not bite and almost do not bark. I have seen in a shop a fishing rod with a hook so beautiful that the largest fish could be caught with it. They are also sold in the first order shotgun stores, like your lord's. They should cost very expensive, at least one hundred rubles each. In the butchers, they sell partridges, hares, rabbits, and it is not known where they hunt them.

«Grandpa: when they light the Christmas tree in the house of the lords, take a golden nut for me and hide it well. Then, when I go, you will give it to me. Ask Miss Olga Ignatievna; Tell him it's for Vanka. You will see how he gives it to you. »

Vanka sighs again and stares at the window. Remember that every year, on the eve of the party, when you had to find a Christmas tree for the lords, he went to the forest with his grandfather. My God, what a charm! The cold made her cheeks red, but he didn't care. The grandfather, before knocking down the chosen tree, lit the pipe and said some chirigotas about Vanka's icy nose. Young fir trees, covered with frost, seemed, in their immobility, to wait for the ax that one of the grandfather's hand should unload on one of them. Suddenly, jumping over the piles of snow, a hare appeared in a rush. The grandfather, seeing her, showed signs of great agitation and, bending down, shouted:"

Take it, take it!" Ah, devil!

Then the grandfather knocked down a fir tree, and between them, they moved him to the manor house. There, the tree was prepared for the party. Miss Olga Ignatievna put more enthusiasm than anyone in this job. Vanka loved her very much. When his mother still lived and served in the house of the lords, Olga Ignatievna gave him chocolates and taught him to read, to write, to count from one to one hundred, and even to dance. But, after his mother died, the orphan Vanka became part of the culinary servitude, with his grandfather, and then was sent to Moscow, to the house of the shoemaker Alajin, to learn the trade...

«Come, grandpa, come! He continued writing, after a short reflection, the boy. In the name of Our Lord, I beg you to get me out of here. Have mercy on the poor orphan. Everyone hits me, makes fun of me, and insults me. And besides, I'm always hungry. And besides, I get bored atrociously and do nothing but cry. The day before yesterday, the mistress gave me such a heavy fish that I fell, and I was not able to get up for a while. This is not living; Dogs live better than me ... Regards to Cook Alena, coachman Egorka and all our friends in the village. My accordion keeps it well, and don't leave it to anyone. Without further

Ado, you know that your grandson VANKA CHUKOV loves you.

Come quickly, Grandpa. »

Vanka folded the sheet of paper in four folds and put it in an envelope he had bought the day before. Then, he meditated a little and wrote on the envelope the following address:

"In the village to my grandfather."

After a new meditation, he added:

"Constantine Makarich."

Congratulating himself on having written the letter without anyone getting in the way, he put on his cap, and, without another coat, ran to the street.

The butcher's clerk, whom he had asked that afternoon, had told him that the letters should be thrown into the mailboxes, where they were collected to take them in troika throughout the world.

Vanka threw her precious epistle into the nearest mailbox...

An hour later, she slept, rocked by sweet hopes.

He saw in dreams of the warm village stove. Sitting on it, her grandfather read Vanka's letter to the cooks. The Snake dog was walking around the stove and wagging his tail...

Chapter13: Palawan

I once went island hopping around Palawan in the Philippines with my friend Sarah. The boat that we rode in was a strange contraption that somewhat resembled one of those large bugs that seem to be able to run across water at lightning speed. Imagine a run of the mill tourist boat with waterski legs that jut out on either side, cutting through the already glass-like sea.

The moment that we set sail toward our destination, my eyes were on the rough mountains on the horizon and beautiful blue water beneath us. The sound of the waves splashing against our vessel as it bobbed around could have put me to sleep after waking up so early this morning.

Our first destination included a long stroll over a rustic boardwalk, the already empty boats that aligned along this dock were wobbling in the waves. The mountains that surrounded us looked to be the sort of structures that begin as blocks of limestone, only for the wind and water to sculpt to their own eye. The Philippines seems like paradise to me. There is a brand of magic pulsing through the veins of some places, and you would be hard-pressed to put it into words, but I will do my best.

As we walked along the trails, we were greeted by pools of the same transparent water, allowing us to see to the bottom. The jagged mountain faces were a dark grey, which allowed for a feeling of real isolation as we continue along our journey. We were walking our way to an absolutely stunning lagoon, the two of us decided to take a dip. The most important part about Palawan is that there are touristy attractions like underwater caves and popular beaches, and they coexist beside parts unknown. We made the decision to visit El Nido (a popular destination) and stay elsewhere in a more relaxing environment.

We spent the rest of our day walking around the various towns of Palawan and taking in the scenery. I even got the chance to dive and witness a clownfish in its natural habitat. I had never seen water so clear and blue. In the movies, when someone is in paradise, this is the place that comes to mind. The people here are

So polite and make every effort to make you feel welcome in their environment.

We arrived back at our wooden hut rental that happened to be in an isolated area right on the white sandy beaches. I stumbled inside the mostly open structure, ready to take a nap after all of the adventuring that we had done today. Sarah said that she would go to the next town to find food while I rested for a bit. It's like the idea struck me all of a sudden that I should take my nap in the hammock outside. The sun was starting to become that less stable orange color that it seems to fade to just before twilight.

I dropped myself down in the hammock, rocking back and forth with unsteadiness at first. Once I discovered my balance again, I laid back to watch the world around me change. The island was the perfect temperature to just hang out in your bathing suit, which I was still wearing. The sea breeze was causing my hair to dance around. The smell of this ocean is something that you can't find anywhere else. Something about the saltwater mixing with the vegetation on the mountains. The only way that I can describe it is the rain in the forest mixed with brackish water.

I was relaxing back in the hammock and watching the fishing boats in the distance, as they appeared to be moving back and forth across their boats. The sound of the waves hitting the perfect sandy beaches was lulling me into a cozy and exotic dream as the sun was sinking behind the horizon and casting its light show along the clouds. I am not even sure how long I was asleep because I did not hear Sarah come back.

When she returned, we ate a delicious meal that was prepared by a local shop in town. It was fresh-caught fish, probably from the boats that I was watching earlier. We ate until we were both really full and very satisfied.

The sun had gone down by this time, and we began to notice that we could see almost every star. The night sky was one of the most impressive things that we have seen since our arrival, especially viewing it from such a lovely location. Sarah and I sat in the sand at the tide in front of our hut and watched as the moon rose above us. I had no words for this moment. This was an almost spiritual moment for me, and I had never felt so relaxed and so in tune with nature.

Sarah and I were mostly silent that night, in the way that most people are after a life-changing experience. We had walked along the stunning snowy looking sand. We had walked the trails among the beautiful lush green mountains, and we had found ourselves conversing with the guides and locals. The lovely coral and exotic fish had captured our imaginations as we floated out among the boldly colored oceanic wildlife. The Philippines has to be one of the most naturally beautiful and tranquil places in the world.

Chapter14: King Tattlemeanie becomes Tattlelaughie

In the far, faraway lands of the Elves, there lived a mean and unkind Elf king named, Tattlemeanie. He was by far the meanest elf who ever lived. He was the king that all the mother Elves warned their kids to run away from and he was the king whom all the kings of the Elves and Fairies in lands far away kept their princesses away from. This king was so mean, even his wives ran away from him. They were terribly scared of him. At one time, one of his queens had forgotten to bring his food at the time she should have brought it. The king first became hungry, and then he became angry; furious. He screamed and yelled very mean words at the queen, and she burst into tears. She was so sad throughout that day, and to make matters worse, the king commanded his mean soldiers to lock her up till she was even more depressed and sorry for what she had done.

"Nobody messes with Tattlemeanie!" He yelled at the top of his voice. Then he turned to his other wives, who hid their scared faces behind the palms of their hands and he yelled, "If you try that with me, I will not just lock you up, I will send you and all your kids into the dark forest, and that is where you will live for the rest of your lives! Do you hear me?". All his wives were shaking with fear, and they were so terrified that they could not even catch their breaths much less speak. They all wept as they watched their fellow queen being dragged off. "How could someone be so mean?" Nobody understood why the king was always so angry and why he loved to make others feel sad every chance he got. It was as if it brought him happiness to see others unhappy; what a really mean king.

Each morning, King Tattlemeanie would wake up early to walk to the place where his servants used to sleep. He loved to hear them talk bad about him so that he would be able to punish them! At night, he would also sneak around to eavesdrop at the doors of the queen's maids so that he would find someone to punish. One day, while he was walking around, pretending to be busy watching beautiful flowers, he overheard a maid talking with another behind the bushes.

They were saying "I really wish that we could have another king, one who will be as kind as King Tattlemeanie's father was. I really don't understand how his father was so kind, and he is so mean to everyone. I want all of us to be as happy as we used to be, I want to live as freely and without fear as before". King Tattlemeanie did not even get angry at all when he heard this; instead, he was happy that he would be able to punish these maids, in the worst way possible, and he did! He sent the two maids as well as their families, into the dark forest, and he told them never to return to the land of the Elves!

That made everyone even more scared of him! And everybody stopped talking about Tattlemeanie, because they did not want to be sent to the dark forest where mean giants lived, and there was little food and water. Even the villagers did not talk about Tattlemeanie, he was indeed the meanest Elf who ever lived!

Once in an Elf month, king Tattlemeanie, his chiefs, soldiers, and the maids, went hunting. He loved to hunt for little birds with his little arrows. He would catch as many birds as he could by shooting at and hurting their wings, so they would not be able to fly, and King Tattlemeanie would then take them to his palace, where he would keep them, and he would have a good laugh at how they all tried to escape from the cage.

It was that time of the month when he went on his hunt, and everyone at the palace was happy, they would finally have some peace and happiness, even if it were only for a few elf days! They all hoped and prayed that he would not change his mind.

Finally, the day arrived, and all the queens and their children watched from the palace windows as he left riding on the back of a huge black bird while his chiefs, soldiers and maids flew as fast as they could trying to catch up with him.

By the time they arrived at the forest, they were all out of breath, but king Tattlemeanie would not allow them to rest, in fact, he scolded them for arriving later than he did and he got angry that they were so out of breath and he yelled, "You bunch of lazy Elves!" Then the hunting began.

That day, king Tattlemeanie decided that he would catch forty birds! And there were only about thirty birds left, he had caught all the others and taken them to his palace. All the others began to get nervous, they knew that if King Tattlemeanie could not capture all of the birds he wanted, they would be in big trouble. He would start shooting his arrows at them, and as they all ran all over trying to escape from the arrows, king Tattlemeanie would have a good laugh. So, they hoped and prayed that he would catch all the birds he wanted or that he would change his mind.

Back at the palace, there was a huge celebration going on, they were all enjoying their freedom away from king Tattlemeanie. They all wished that he never returned or that something happened and he would return as a kind person, even kinder than his father had been! They had no idea that one of their wishes would be granted! But which of the two wishes?

Back at the forest, king Tattlemeanie had caught only twenty birds, and he was getting more and more upset as there seemed to be no birds left in the forest. "I want all forty birds, and I want them now", he shrieked as he stomped his foot on the ground and pulled at his hair like a kid. He pushed the other Elves around, yelling at them to bring the birds to him; if they did not, he would cage them all up and have some fun as he watched them try to escape.

All the maids had begun to cry like babies, and the soldiers were all swearing. The chiefs had their leaf caps in their hands and stammered as they tried to calm the king down.

On a tree nearby, an old fairy watched, "What a mean king this is!" she thought. She flew off the tree and went down to stand right in front of King Tattlemeanie. King Tattlemeanie was startled for about two seconds. He was shocked that the old fairy would dare to even come close to him without being instructed to do so. Even his chiefs wouldn't dare!

"Who are you old? Ugly, looking fairy?" He asked with his face all squeezed up in disgust. The fairy chuckled and said, "I'm your master, you mean King!" the fairy responded. King Tattlemeanie was so shocked that he started stammering, "M..my..my..mas...master? You called me, mean? Mean! Mean!! Mean!!! Oh I'm going to show you what being mean means, you just wait right here!"

The fairy watched calmly as king Tattlemeanie ran and tripped over his own boots about three times in his struggle to get to his bow and arrow and his large bird. The others watched helplessly as all these happened. The fairy burst into laughter as Tattlemeanie kept falling off his bird and then finally he gave up and grabbed his arrows. He kept on firing the arrows at the old fairy, but each time he missed. He became even angrier when she flew up high, way out of his reach, as he could not fly so high. She was also way faster than he was, and she was laughing really hard as she saw how angry the King was. Even the chiefs had forgotten about their fear and were beginning to laugh while covering their faces with their caps. King Tattlemeanie felt otherwise though, he was so angry that he was close to tears, and he just might start shedding tears at any moment!

At one point, he stopped and yelled, "If it's the last thing I do, I'll make sure I catch you today!". Then the old fairy answered, "No, catching me won't be the last thing you do, laughing is the last thing you will do". Then, the old fairy reached into the side of her left-wing and brought out a wand; the wand was small and shiny. She held it up and then rolled it thrice and said, "Tattlemeanie shall become Tattlelaughie, and he shall laugh till the end of his elf life!"

"Ha! Laugh? I never laugh old fairy, certainly not now! I..." Tattlemeanie was saying, but he did not get to finish that thought because he started to laugh! He was laughing so hard, big tears were in his eyes and every time he tried to say mean things he laughed! When he kept quiet, he stopped, then he tried to say mean things to the others Elves' instead, he began to laugh again. He laughed so hard, he could not stand straight.

When he saw that this would not stop, he tried to beg the fairy. Then, all of a sudden, he found himself talking again. "There you go, you will only get to say nice things, but if you want to say mean things, you shall laugh instead!" the fairy said and flew off. The new King Tattlelaughie then quietly got on his bird and flew off. That day was the last time King Tattlelaughie said any mean words to anyone. Everyone became happy at the palace and even in the village, and they all lived happily ever after, but as for King Tattlelaughie, he lived happily ever laughter!

Chapter15:Tranquility

It was four in the afternoon on a Saturday, and the sun was perched lazily above the trees. I had grown bored of sitting in my house, so I decided to walk to the local park and sit at a bench instead and watch people around me enjoying their lives. When I arrived, the park was bustling with young families playing, lovers holding hands, and individuals jogging or biking around the perimeter of the park. It was a busy day, as everyone was enjoying the late summer sunshine before it went away for another season.

All around, people were enjoying the day as much as they could. When I had sat down, I admired a few young families that were running around together playing Frisbee. Their younger children were running wild, without a care in the world. It was clear that they were too young to truly understand the concept of Frisbee; so instead, they chased their parents around the grass and laughed each time they would turn on their heels and tumble to the ground. The older children were rather competitive, fighting over who was scoring the most points and who would come out as the winner of this game of Frisbee. The parents were playing, although they were playing with much less concern than the children. They did not care who was winning or losing, they were simply helping show their children how to throw the Frisbee and catch it properly.

In another direction, a lovely couple had arrived and were holding hands and giggling as they slowly followed the path through the park. They were not making much grounds, as they would stop every so often to hug, kiss, and enjoy each other's presence. The smiles on their faces said it all, as they were clearly in the process of falling deeply in love with each other. I smiled as they continued walking through the park without a care in the world for anyone or anything around them. I remembered back to when my wife and I were younger and falling in love, and I quietly thanked them for bringing back these long since gone memories to my elderly mind. I smiled at the thought of how beautiful it was to enjoy such times together with our loved ones.

As I leaned back on the bench, a young man jogged in front of me, making his way down the trail. He seemed to be listening to some fairly loud music as he ran by, likely to help keep him focused and make the process more enjoyable. I watched as he breathed rhythmically, keeping his breaths focused and making steady progress through the park. Eventually, he reached the end of the trail and took off down the sidewalk, likely heading back home from his afternoon jog.

As I sat in the park and looked around me, I realized that all around me life was bustling and yet I was sitting, undisturbed, in my quiet little space on the bench. Every now and again someone would smile and wave at me as they walked past, but otherwise, I was simply alone and enjoying the moment. I closed my eyes for a brief moment and breathed in deeply, smelling the sweet summer air that was all around. When I opened them up again,

I took a moment to look past all of the people and see the park itself. Trees edged the pathway on the distant side of the park, and only grass and small bushes here and there lined it the rest of the way. There were benches every so often, as well as a few garbage cans with waste stations for people who had brought their dogs around. Behind me, a luscious community garden was rich with flowers and vegetables. It was filled with bumble bees and butterflies that were enjoying the gentle breeze that helped them glide from flower to flower, and plant to plant.

I sat for several more minutes, enjoying the tranquility of the moment and feeling into the peace of it all. In my younger years, times like this did not mean much to me. I was more likely to be the couple laughing and falling in love, or the Dad teaching his children how to throw a Frisbee through the park so that they could enjoy a fun game together. I may have even been the man jogging at one point, far before I had ever met my wife or had kids with her. It was fascinating to see the tranquil reality of all different stages of life spread out before me.

When I was done sitting, I grabbed my cane from the bench and stood up, placing it on the ground beneath my feet. I could hear the gravel crunching beneath my feet and cane as I slowly made my way back home, where I would sit in the living room and admire the pictures of my wife and kids and remember the life we once shared together. There, I would be alone too, and I would experience an entirely different type of tranquil compared to the lively and bright one at the park.

Chapter16: Catching Up

Hannah browsed the social media website idly for far longer than she had ever intended to. And she could feel her work emails starting to pile up while she continued to procrastinate. She wasn't sure what all the emails were about, but she was well aware that it was something she wouldn't want to deal with at least until she had gotten to finish her current cup of coffee. She continued to watch videos of terribly-conceived life hacks, overly decadent recipe videos, and pictures of babies she would likely never get to meet.

In her browsing, she happened to stumble on the name of an old friend with whom she had lost contact some years ago. Tanya and Hannah had been an inseparable duo from the very beginning of middle school, all the way through senior year of high school. Something happened to end that friendship rather suddenly, but she couldn't for the life of her remember what that had been. She thought about the times Tanya had come to stay at her house and helped her to terrorize Hannah's little brother.

On a lark, she sent a request to add Tanya to her list of friends on the social media site. Within minutes, Tanya had accepted the request and sent an excited message to Hannah.

Oh, my goodness, Hannah Fischer!

How have you been; it's been so long since I've gotten to see you!

Are you still living in the area?

Hannah was so happy to see that Tanya had been just as eager to reconnect as Hannah had been and sent her response immediately.

Yes! I'm still in the area; are you?

I would love to meet for coffee if you're not too busy. Maybe tomorrow at the coffee place off route 30?

Seconds later, her reply came.

Yes! Let's do that tomorrow. Does 2:00 work for you?

The date was set. Hannah would meet with her old best friend in less than 24 hours. She looked forward to catching up, reminiscing, and laughing about their exploits.

The next day, they arrived at the coffee shop right on time and hugged in the parking lot.

"My God, Tanya! You look amazing; I can't believe how long it's been since we've touched base and how amazing you look in spite of the time that's passed!"

"Oh, my gosh you're too nice. Are you kidding me, look at you? You look fantastic!"

The two got their coffees and picked a table where they could sit to do their catching up.

"How have you been, Hannah? What's going on in your life these days?"

"I'm doing really well, actually. I'm working on getting a promotion in my job as a front-end web developer for a tech company that works downtown."

"That's so great! You were always so good at the technological stuff. That's why I had you come over to help me fix the VCR after—"

"After Jonah put bubblegum in it! I remember; I had to take that whole thing apart and clean it with a toothbrush before I could put it back together!"

"I was so glad you did that, too. My dad would have absolutely killed me if he found out I was on the phone with Parker and not watching him when it happened."

"We were always getting each other out of messes like that, though! We were ride or die for each other and that was how it was always going to be. I remember when we said we were going to start a band. My mom lamented about the loud music in the garage and my brother wouldn't stop laughing at the name we had chosen. What was it again?"

"The Block Knockers," Tanya said, placing a palm squarely on her forehead, laughing with embarrassment. "I cannot believe we thought that was a good idea."

"I think we tried to make t-shirts with puffy paint at one point."

"You're right, I remember Mittens stepping in it and getting it on the carpet." They both laughed heartily at the memory.

"I can't even remember why we stopped being friends. It's so nice to catch up and talk about those days!" Tanya sipped awkwardly at her coffee. "Oh no; do I want to know what it was that did it? Did I completely stick my foot in my mouth?" Hannah looked nervous as Tanya slowly put her coffee down on the table.

"Marcus Hughes," was all Tanya said and Hannah clapped a hand to her mouth.

"Oh, my God; you're right. I had such a ridiculous crush on him. When you kissed him first, I blew a gasket!" Tanya nodded with her teeth gritted.

"Teenage girls can get ugly over boys, man." Hannah placed her palms on her cheeks and grimaced.

"I can't believe I cut you off for that. I can't believe I threw away seven years of friendship over a kiss!" Tanya hadn't wanted to rub any of this in Hannah's face, but she felt she needed to let her know everything that happened.

"You told me that I ruined your self-esteem and you accused me of stealing your one chance at happiness," Tanya said through a pained grimace. Hannah reached out and grabbed Tanya's hand, feeling awful about what she had said.

"I remember that now. I remember feeling like Marcus was my own shot at true love... Which was ridiculous, because I think I had spoken to him twice. God, I am so sorry about that. What a ridiculous thing to say!"

"Honestly, it's all water under the bridge. I was so happy when you reached out; I figured you had finally found in your heart to forgive me for swooping in on the boy you liked."

"You didn't swoop! He kissed you first and you guys liked each other! By all accounts, I was horning in on your good time, and I am absolutely the witch in this story." Tanya laughed and disagreed.

"I'm so glad that you're not mad about this anymore. You know, after you and I stopped hanging out, I didn't stop seeing Marcus right away."

"Oh, really? Was he a good boyfriend? I hope he was. He always seemed like such a good guy," Hannah said.

"You know, he was a really, really good boyfriend. In fact, I loved dating him so much, I said yes when he asked me to marry him about three years later." Hannah's jaw dropped.

"You married Marcus Hughes! Wow! I'm so happy for you both. Have you both been doing really well since high school?"

"We really have! Marcus owns his own business and I help him run it. We have been having better and better earnings each year for the last three, and we're looking at expanding outside of our home office this year!" The girls continued catching up, telling stories, and enjoying one another's company.

At the end of the day, an old friendship had been rekindled and it was as though two sisters had reunited. They were just as comfortable as they had ever been with one another.

Chapter17: The Lost Woods

I sat at the balcony of my uncle's house when a tall, skinny old man dressed in rags limped past me and rang the doorbell. For a millisecond, I thought he was blind after all he seemed to walk in a haphazard fashion and didn't seem to acknowledge the presence of someone sitting right beside the door he was knocking, but he wasn't, his precision to the position of the doorbell said affirmed that. My uncle came for the door, and the old man asked for shelter for the night, who wouldn't help an old, hungry man – well, not my uncle. Once the man got in and ate the meal offered him by my aunt, he looked at the kids and said he had a story for them, they were excited. From the balcony, I listened too. I was bored. For some reason, my uncle and aunt seemed to listen. He got us all hooked.

"Once upon a time", he stated, "There lived a young man, Brad, he was a college graduate and a training boxer, but didn't seem to make the cut in his boxing career. Years of training didn't seem to be paying off and he was getting frustrated. His coach had just told him to go get a life outside boxing as he might never make a successful boxer. Dejected, he slung his bag across his shoulders and walked all the way home. His rent was due. His girlfriend, Lucy, was getting frustrated with his incessant failures. He was crossroads and thoughts of suicide crossed his mind.

On getting home, he met a delivery man at his door. He shrugged, signed and received the mail he had come to deliver. Opening it, he saw the surprise of his life. The best news of his life – or the worst. His grand-uncle had just passed away and he was to inherit his estate in a small, old town called Old Town. The mail also contained the password to a safe said to contain an unspecified sum of money. "Gosh! My life had been transformed, I'm rich!!!", he screamed excitedly.

Before dawn the next day, they were blaring loud music in Jake's car and singing excitedly on their way to Old Town. In the car with Lucy, Jake, and Rick, his best buddies. They busted speed limits in euphoria, and before noon, they were in Old Town, but out of gasoline. They took a break to ask a few locals to point them in the exact direction of Brad's new estate, but they got a very unexpected reply. It was located a few meters into a 'forbidden' forest and they were advised not to venture into the forest. Some even begged them passionately. An old man said legend has it that the forest is said to house the corpse of 10,000 slaves who were beheaded and buried alongside an ancient great ruler. And the forest seems to be eternally haunted by the ghosts of the slain slaves and whoever goes in never returns alive. As soon as he finished speaking, he walked away briskly.

They were all startled and glued to the spot – all except Lucy. She was a staunch atheist and had zero belief for superstition and spirituality. She laughed loudly and heartily. 'This is some scary bedtime story told to stubborn kids to force them to sleep', she said. Brad and Jake laughed, Rick feigned a smile, but he was really freaked out.

Nevertheless, they ventured in. Drove into the forest excitedly and everything looked normal. They made jokes about the local's warming and laughed heartily. 'Holy sh*t, this is heaven', Lucy said. They drove in and explored the estate. A real big property. It was serene, peaceful and beautiful. They felt relaxed. Rick too.

At the time they finished touring the estate, it was dusk and they decided to stay the night at the estate. Rick, the geek, decided to tour the mansion with a drone to discover new things. Brad and Lucy stayed up watching TV while Jake just read a book. It was Rick who was the first to sense the presence of paranormal activity. While exploring the mansion through the eyes of his drone, a shadowy figure quickly moved past the camera – or so he thought. His mind was playing a fast one on him, he shrugged it off and continued his surf.

At the nick of 10:00 p.m., the entire atmosphere seemed to change, the audible eerie sound of unidentifiable creatures seemed to fill the air and even Lucy got scared. She cuddled up with Brad, but not for long. A loud scream jerked them off the bed and they immediately ran into the sitting room to see what had happened. Jake ran into the sitting room too, but Rick wasn't. In his place, they saw blood. Blood dragged across the sitting room and trailed into the next room. Jake immediately peed on his pants. Their hearts were racing faster than a lightning bolt. Lucy courageously trailed the blood, which terminated in the other room with the most grotesque sight she had ever seen. It was Rick's body, unmistakably, albeit without ahead. "Apparently, his head had been crushed, but by who?" Lucy asked. Loud laughter from nowhere, in particular, was the reply she got for her question. It dawned on them that they were in some creepy house.

They all ran into one of the rooms, locked all doors and windows, cuddled close and tightly closed their eyes, but sleep was far away. Brad silently prayed to make it to the next morning then run off with all the money in the safe, sell off the house and live lavishly for the rest of his life. The eerie sounds intensified with intermittent laughter. Then their room door opened on its own, this time, Brad prayed to just make it to the next day and vowed to leave all the money and donate the house to charity. The door stayed open, their hearts in their mouths, then it shut with a loud bang. And tranquility was returned, it was 6:00 a.m.

At the first sunray, they hurriedly packed their belongings, opened the safe and took more money than they could count. They loaded it into the car trunk, zoomed off and bade the house farewell.

Four hours later, they were still trying to find their way out of the Forest. The ride from the City to the estate lasted less than twenty minutes. They seemed to be moving in circles, the forest seemed to be an unsolvable maze. The sun was setting, their gas got exhausted and they still hadn't found their way out. They walked on foot for hours, abandoning the money. It was after they got tired that they realized they have been revolving two trees all day. Then the old man's word came to mind; "Whoever goes in, never comes back alive". Panic set in.

The much-dreaded nightfall, once again. The cold breeze seemed to have a voice of its own and seemed to whistle a song of death. They made the long journey back home, they were scared to death. They started hearing brisk footsteps behind them, and they started walking faster than the footsteps increased accordingly. They were now running at full throttle, Brad was leading the pack when he heard a loud thud right at his back. Jake had fallen. He slipped on a rock and smashed his head on a rock. E wiggled his body for some seconds and gave up the ghost. Lucy just humped over him and ran into the house, while Brad stood motionless for a while before moving in.

Lucy was wearing a helmet when Brad got in, and she handed Brad another helmet. He put it on before asking why 'the spirits seem to be after our heads, Jake and Rick died from head wounds', she said. Brad just looked on blankly.

That night, they cuddled up and shut their eyes once again hoping to catch some sleep, they muffed their ears to block off the spooky sounds. Somehow, Brad slept off some hours later and woke up to the creepiest thing he had ever seen, he was cuddling a headless Lucy. Her head was gently placed on the side table, with both her helmet and his on her lifeless head. He just burst out laughing with tears gushing down his eyes. He knew it was game over for him and wished he had died earlier. And he eventually died." That is the end of my story, said the tall, skinny, old man.

This is actually a true story, he added. It was personally written by Brad, shortly before he died. The last line of the story as written by Brad read "If you're reading this, you're probably in the forbidden forest and might not make it out alive too". I read it from the forest and Brad was right. I didn't make it out alive. Yes! I'm a ghost, as he said this, his head fell off. All I heard were screams, I dashed off. And that was the last I saw of my uncle and his family.

Chapter 18: Saleh

Saleh woke up to the warmth around him. He tried stretching, but he winced in pain. The last thing he could remember was being knocked off by an ice golem. Dariel twirled her fingers around his black hair as she nursed him back to health.

"You're up!" She said with excitement in her voice. Dariel had never seen a human and the idea of having one around totally fascinated her. She gave him soup and helped him sit up as he ate. Just then, Vulen stepped in with his catch for the day. His archery skills were second to none. He had a pout on his lips as he stared at Saleh who said hello to him almost immediately. He nodded his head as if observing his environment. Vulen was weary of humans. "Only Santa Claus is nice", he always argued. "He'll leave as soon as he is fine", Dariel said defensively without being asked.

Saleh got better as the days went by. One day, Dariel asked him, "Why were you in the mountains?" Dariel possessed so much calmness. Her beautiful hair glistened under the sun as he told her about his mission to save Faland. "Why do you stay here? I thought elves don't stay on mountains" Saleh asked innocently. "We're mountain elves," she replied sweetly. He told her a lot of things. His problems challenges he faced and even told her about the plan with Gargoth, a huge man with a few strands of hair at the center of his head. Saleh excitedly talked about how great

Gargoth was. Dariel looked at him with sadness on her face. "How did you kill the golem?" he asked as he was filled with curiosity. Dariel waved the question off by excusing herself. Saleh got well and wanted to leave the mountain top. He gave the elves a bag of gold coins, which they refused to take. "How do I reward you?" he asked. "Just keep yourself safe," Vulen said as he shot a bird with his arrow.

"You just can't leave yet!" Dariel said to him with concern written all over her. Her porcelain skin was so beautiful! It complemented her long, beautiful hair. "But why?" Saleh asked confusedly. "You have to learn to fight, to be safe and to protect yourself". "Dariel's Right!" Vulen added and paused "We wouldn't always be there to protect you," he said as he shrugged his shoulders and walked away. "To be a hero, there are lots of obstacles lots of monsters, but with knowledge on the right things, you'll prevail", Dariel said as she sewed.

Saleh made up his mind to stay and learn. Riches weren't enough for him, he just wanted to save Faland from all her oppressors. The goblins that ate the kids up, the one-eyed crows that invaded their farms, the heartless humans who took from the poor to enrich themselves all of them. The sun went down and Vulen asked Saleh to come with him to the woods, he taught him how to aim and shoot. Saleh was devoted and, soon, with so much practice, he was almost as good as Vulen.

Gorgoth was so excited because Saleh didn't return. He wore a gladiator sandal and went around bullying everyone. He was only nice because he wanted to deceive the town's savior Saleh into going away to the mountains so he can be killed by the dangerous creatures there.

Vulen and Saleh went to the woods to shoot. At noon, Dariel came with some snacks she made for them. For every aim that was hit on target, she divulged an important survival nugget to Saleh. "Trust no one", "Completely distinguish your enemies from your friends" "Never disclose your plans to anyone", she said to him firmly. Evening came and they retired home.

"I'll teach you magic and how to cast spells," Dariel said to him with a straight face. "But I can cast spells," Saleh said in defense. "That isn't enough", Vulen said as he left the shelter. Dariel taught Saleh many magical tricks, improved his ability to cast spells. When you want to kill an enemy, look into his eyes and strike him in the heart. It rang like a bell in his ears.

Time passed and Saleh had to go. It was a sad goodbye. He had become part of them. They walked him to the end of the mountains and bade him farewell. "You can always come home," they said to him in unison. He nodded and a teardrop on his brown cheek. "Goodbye," he said and walked away occasionally looking back to see them again.

The whole town was in disarray. People ran helter-skelter. "Ghost!" some of them screamed locking their doors tightly as they saw Saleh. Gorgoth told them he was dead and his corpse was eaten by vultures. Saleh felt so sad and went to see Gorgoth who was dining with the oppressors, he claimed to also dread. His face turned green and his mouth was agape. He didn't expect Saleh to return. "Come take this man to jail," Gandhi, one of the oppressors said to the soldiers and everyone burst into laughter.

At that spot, Saleh killed half of them with his bow and arrow staring deeply into their eyes. It took half of the soldiers to capture Saleh and put him behind bars. The night passed and morning came. Saleh wasn't in the cell. He was searched for, but wasn't found. He had cast a spell on everyone there to sleep off as he magically took the keys out of the jailer's pocket. "I'll kill Gorgoth and hang his head on the city gates" he swore. He marched to Gorgoth's home. A defenseless Gorgoth appeared before him asking why he wasn't in jail. "Because I'm here to kill you", he replied. Gorgoth laughed hard and Saleh looked at Gorgoth in his eyes and struck an arrow to his chest.

Everyone around ran in fear. He took a sword from the guards and cut Gorgoth's head off. The news spread and all the bad people fled in fear. Gorgoth's head was embalmed and placed on the city gate. The people cheered in excitement and crowned Saleh king. Occasionally, he visited the elves and took to them a lot of food. Saleh felt fulfilled. Faland was happy and peaceful ever after.

Chapter19: A Day at the Beach

You have taken a day off to spend at the beach. You are alone, and feel totally comfortable in your own skin. Around you are large crowds, but they feel very far away from you, and their presence does not overwhelm you in the slightest. There is a bubble around you, and, in fact, the presence of the crowd is uplifting, both in its juxtaposition with yourself, and in its own self-sustainability. These crowds of people are happy and loving and having the greatest times of their lives, and they are totally independent of you, and need nothing from you, as you need nothing from them. There is a great peace in this that you feel, a calm that there could be so much right in the world that exists totally without any need from you. It is inspiring and uplifting, and makes you feel free. The presence of the crowds does absolutely nothing to affect your ability to enjoy the natural pleasures of the beach. It seems as if the crowd has parted perfectly to allow you the best view possible of the shore and the horizon. You wonder how far out the water is visible. It could be one mile, or a hundred. To you, what you are seeing seems infinite, and infinitely calm. You feel as if you could walk across the beach and into the water and drift forever into the void of this great blue mass, and there would be no end in sight. At the edge of what is visible to you, the sky opens up, being an even greater and holier chasm, the abyss of the sea spread exponentially into the universe. It is amazing to you to watch these two divine forces, reflections of each other, connect and touch and embrace. It is you, yourself, embracing the infinite. The sand around you, likewise, is infinite, being an infinite number of grains. Every handful that you pick up and allow to pass through your fingers is infinity, a universe of universes. You are humbled by the sheer number of particles that make up this small space within your bubble, and in it's close proximity your mind wanders exponentially to the infinities lying elsewhere, within the other infinities, the small, personal spaces that make up our existence, and the endless number of spaces there can be. You are melting into the ground through your beach towel, as every particle of you intermingles with the endless particles in the sand, and every particle in your soul floats into the breeze towards the shore, interspersing through the waters until they end their journey at the horizon, at which point the dust will float up through the heavens, and eternity. You are melting, sinking, and your mind is leaving your body. Time slows down inside of your bubble as it speeds up among those crowds that had once been around you, now light-years away. Generations come and go among the beach crowds, as you remain perfectly still, and content, a part of something greater than yourself, yet which is only great because of yourself, the infinity. An eternity passes and you are back on the beach. You get up, the beach air bringing new life back into your lungs, and your blood, and your body, and your mind. Your eyes gaze anew upon the sight as you make your way towards the water, through the path that has been cleared by the universe through this large, intangible crowd that seems totally unaware of your presence. It is an infinite and joyous walk to the shore, and feels like walking towards the light, towards the afterlife. You feel the sand become wet at your feet, and where the particles once brushed up into the crevices of your feet and fell through, now they are molding into you, a larger mass, bonded by the water, each step leaving an impression in the sand which welcomes you with open arms, like a slipper that fits just right. Eventually, your feet feel the total submersion into the water, and the sand totally beneath. Instantly, you are connected most tangibly to the entire whole. Whereas you were always a part of this abyss, now it has awakened within you tenfold, and upon first touch you feel the water connecting to the sky at the horizon, connecting to the heavens above. There is only blue, a great, blue abyss, a serenity that perpetuates outwards for eternity. You continue, and continue to be submerged. As the water goes up above your waistline, you feel your entire body become weightless. You look back and see the crowds, and it feels as if you are in space looking back down onto the planet from which you came. In a beautiful way, the people on the beach seem like insects, and you feel totally removed from any part of them. The void behind you is what you feel the closest kinship with; it's infinite stretches and unending silence and space. You fall back into the water, and as it touches your head your mind melts away into this endless sea of blue. You are now flowing, totally weightless, into the abyss. You float for what seems like hours, then days, then weeks, then months, then years, then a lifetime, then further generations down, but it is only a second. This continues for a long while before you have reached that horizon, that point that you saw back on the beach where the blue of the waters transcended into the blue of the sky. With this meeting, you transcend as well, as your entire being transmutes into the air, becoming the glowing golden clouds of the sunset. You are as large as the entire visible sky, looking down at the place you came from, glowing golden between the earth and the heavens. For an eternity, the sun sits at the horizon, projecting you onto the clouds, the golden glow of your soul. As it fades, your consciousness fades, and the whole of your golden glow becomes broken into infinite pieces, becoming the multitude of stars in the sky. Now you are in space, divided amongst the cosmos, neither here nor there, in infinite black. You are totally still, you are the night sky, and you are asleep.

Chapter 20: Joy

Ruth was an elderly lady now, in her mid-seventies. She sat on her patio each morning, overlooking the neighborhood and waving to the people as they walked by. Each morning, children would walk to school and families would walk their dogs, and Ruth would just watch and smile at each one. This time of day was Ruth's favorite, as it reminded her of all of the wonderful things that she had to be joyful about in her lifetime.

Ruth remembered her childhood when she would walk to school with her six siblings and enjoy classes at the schoolhouse. She was not very fond of her teachers, but she loved learning and she loved playing outside with her friends on breaks. She remembered sitting in the grass one afternoon eating a snack her Mom had packed for her and watching the younger kids play hopscotch in the dirt. To Ruth, this was one of her favorite memories that she shared with her siblings because it was so simple and brought so much joy to her life.

Ruth also remembered when she graduated and met her husband, Donald. Donald went straight into the military after school and served the country for nearly half a decade. For that entire time, Ruth raised their family, took care of the home front, and sent letters to Donald every week as she let him know how much she loved him and missed him. She would pour the day to day happenings into the letters, always trying to give Donald a feel of what was going on at home so that he felt like he was not missing out when he was gone. She remembered the sheer joy of seeing Donald for the first time, and for the first time after he returned home from every deployment. It always felt like she was falling in love all over again when he returned home.

Ruth also remembered what it felt like when Donald finally came home and stayed home, as he was done serving in the military. She remembered waking up to him every single day, learning how to live together as a couple, and living in sheer awe of this man who she adored so much. Ruth found so much joy in seeing Donald every day that she always did her best to find the small ways to bring even more joy into their days on a regular basis. Whether it was brewing him coffee when he was tired or slow dancing with him in the kitchen, Ruth loved bringing a smile to Donald's face in any way that she could.

As an older couple walked by holding hands, Ruth remembered the joy she gained from holding hands with Donald all through his life. When they were walking in public, he would always grab her hand in his and lead her around, which helped Ruth feel so cared for and protected. She remembered how strong his hand felt, and how his body always seemed to be positioned in a way where he was ready to protect her if she needed him. Donald was a very protective and caring man, and Ruth always felt so safe in his presence.

Ruth remembered how even when Donald was ill with cancer, he was still so strong and protective until he could no longer be. As he withered away and he found that he was no longer able to physically protect Ruth, he still did his best to mentally and emotionally protect her by comforting her and telling her that everything would be okay. Donald told Ruth how he would watch over her every day so that she could carry on without him, even when she believed that she would never be able to. She was to wake up every day and continue looking for joy in every day, just as she had done since he had come home from the war. Donald told Ruth that she was to brew herself coffee, dance to their favorite songs while she sang quietly to herself, and walk with bravery everywhere she went. This, Donald said, would be the way that she could feel his presence after he left.

Now, nearly twenty years after he had passed, Ruth still found ways to bring herself joy every morning. Part of that joy was in brewing herself a fresh pot of Donald's favorite coffee every morning and sipping a cup on the porch while she watched the families go by, while reminiscing on her own family that had long since grown and left. At night, she would put on their favorite songs and dance, or sing to them as she wiped off her makeup and prepared herself for bed.

As she was preparing to head inside for the day, Ruth saw an elderly couple walking their grandchildren to school. This made Ruth reminisce on her own grandchildren, and what it was like when they visited. When her children came to visit her, Ruth would share her favorite memories of Donald with them, in hopes of keeping his memory alive and introducing him to his grandkids through her memories. She would show them his photographs and watch them in sheer awe of how joyful they were to get to know the man that she had once loved so dearly, and in that she would find joy of her own. Every time, she knew that Donald was right there smiling with them and holding her hand, helping her stay brave whenever she missed him the most.

Chapter21: After The Fair

The fair was already closed, the lights on the stalls where they sold the coconut slices had been turned off, and the little wooden horses, motionless in the dark, awaited the music and the rerun of the machinery that would set them jogging again. In the booths, the mothballs had gone out one by one, and the canvases covered the game boards one by one. The entire crowd had returned home, and there was only a little light left in the caravan windows.

No one had noticed that girl. Leaning on the side of the roundabout, dressed in black completely, I heard the last rumor of the already distant steps that were marked on the sawdust and the murmur of goodbyes. Then, alone in the middle of that desert of horses of profile and humble fantastic boats, he began to look for a place to spend the night. Here and there, raising the canvases that covered the stalls as if they were shrouds, it made its way into the darkness. He was scared of mice running around junk-filled entailments, and he was afraid of the same fluttering of the canvas that the air wobbled like the sails of a ship. He had hidden by the merry-go-round. It slipped inside, and with the creaking of the steps the bells that the horses had hung around their neck rang. He dared not breathe until the quiet silence resumed and the darkness had not forgotten the noise. In all the gondolas, in all the positions I looked with my eyes for a bed to lie on, but there was not a single place in the whole fair where I could go to sleep. Some because they were too quiet, others because of the mice. In the astrologer's post was a pile of straw. He knelt on his side and when he reached out he felt that he was touching a child's hand. In the astrologer's post was a pile of straw. He knelt on his side and when he reached out he felt that he was touching a child's hand. In the astrologer's post was a pile of straw. He knelt on his side and when he reached out he felt that he was touching a child's hand.

No, there wasn't a single place. Slowly, he went to the wagons that were farther from the center of the fair, and discovered that there were lights in only two of them. He held his empty bag tightly and remained undecided while deciding which one he was going to bother. Finally he chose to knock on the window of a small and decrepit one that was there next door. On tiptoe, he looked inside. In front of a kitchenette, toasting a slice of bread, sat the fattest man I had ever seen. He tapped three knuckles on the glass and then hid in the shadows. He heard the man go up the steps and ask: "Who? Who?" But he dared not answer. "Who? Who? "He repeated.

The man's voice, as thin as thick was his body, made him laugh.

And he, upon discovering the laughter, turned to where the darkness hid it.

"First call," he said, "then you hide and then laugh, huh?"

The girl then appeared in a circle of light, knowing that she no longer needed to remain hidden.

"A girl," said the man. Go on, get in and shake your feet.

He didn't even wait for her; He had already retired inside the wagon, and she had no choice but to follow him, climb the steps and get into that messy knife. The man had sat down again and was still toasting the same slice of bread.

-Are you there? He asked, because at that moment he turned his back.

-I close the door? Asked the girl. And he closed it without waiting for an answer.

He sat on a cot and watched him toast the bread.

"I know how to toast bread better than you," said the girl.

"I have no doubt," said the Fat man.

He saw that he placed a piece of charred bread on a plate, and saw that he immediately put another in front of the fire. It burned immediately.

"Let me toast it," she said. And he clumsily extended the fork and the entire bar.

"Cut it," he said, "take it and eat it."

She sat in the chair.

"Look how you have sunk my bed," said the Fat man, "who are you to sink my bed?"

"My name is Annie," he said.

He immediately had all the toast and buttered bread, and the girl arranged it on two plates and brought two chairs to the table.

"I'm going to eat mine in bed," said the Fat man. Take it here.

When they finished dinner, he pushed his chair away and began to contemplate it from the other end of the table.

"I am the Fat," he said. I'm from Treorchy. The fortune teller next door is from Aberdare.

"I'm not from the fair," said the girl. I come from Cardiff.

"Cardiff is a very big city," the Fat man nodded. And asked him why he was there.

"For money," Annie said.

And then he told him things about the fair, the places he had walked, the people he had met. He told him how old he was, what he thought, what his brothers were called and how he would like to put his son. He showed him a postcard of the port of Boston and a portrait of his mother, who was a weightlifter. And he told her what summer was like in Ireland.

"I've always been that fat," he said, "and now I'm already fat." Because I'm so fat, nobody wants to touch me.

He talked about a heat wave in Sicily, he talked about the Mediterranean. She told him about the boy he had found in the astrologer's position.

"That's because of the stars again," he said.

"That child is going to die," Annie said.

He opened the door and went out into darkness. She did not move. He looked around, thinking that maybe he had gone to look for a policeman. It would be a fatality to be caught again by the police. On the other side of the open door, the night was inhospitable and she brought the chair to the kitchen.

"If you are going to catch me, you better get caught hot," he told himself.

From the noise, he knew that the Fat man was approaching and began to tremble. He climbed the steps like a mountain with legs, and she clenched her hands under her skinny chest. Despite the darkness, he saw that the Fat man was smiling.

"Look what the stars have done," he said. He had the astrologer's boy in his arms.

She cradled him. The boy whined in his lap until he was silent. The girl told her the fear that had happened after she left.

"What would I do with a cop?"

She told him that a policeman was looking for her.

"And what have you done to get you looking for the police?"

She did not answer. Only the child was taken to the sterile chest. And he saw how thin she was.

"You have to eat, Cardiff," he said.

And then the boy began to cry. With a groan, the crying began to turn into a storm of despair. The girl rocked it, but nothing could relieve it.

-Shut up, shut up! Said the Fat, but the crying was still increasing. Annie suffocated him with kisses and caresses, but the screams persisted.

"We have to do something," she said.

"Sing her a babysitter."

He did so, but the boy did not like it.

"We can only do one thing," he said. We have to take it to the merry-go-round.

And with the boy hugged around his neck, he hurried down the carriage stairs and ran through the fair, deserted, while the Fat man was panting at his heels.

Between stalls and stalls they reached the center of the fair, where the roundabouts were, and climbed into one of the mounts.

"Start it," she said.

From a distance the Fat man could be heard circling the handlebar with which the mechanism that put the horses to gallop the entire day began to run. She heard the jerky rerun of machinery well. At the foot of the horses, the boards shuddered in a crunch. The girl saw that El Gordo leveraged a crank and saw him sit on the saddle of the smaller horse. The merry-go-round began to spin slowly at first, but quickly gained speed. The boy who was carrying the little girl now didn't cry anymore: he was beating his palms. The air of the night curled his hair, music vibrated in his ears. The little horses kept going round and round, and the trembling of their hooves silenced the wails of the night wind.

And that's how the people of the fair began to come out of their wagons, and thus they found the Fat man and the girl in black who carried a little boy in his arms. In their mechanical steeds they circled and more laps, to the beat of an organ music that was increasing.

Chapter22: The Dragon and the Wind

More momentum! "Arthuro looked down a little anxiously from the top of the mountain. He was a 2-meter-long, blue-green dragon with bright yellow eyes, large silver spines - and today he practiced flying with his dad. But it was a bit more difficult than he thought: what if he fell from the air and broke a wing?

"Arthur, more momentum!" Arthur and his dad were practicing Arthur's new paper kite down the mountain. It just did not work out because the wind did not blow so hard and Arthur had to walk really fast, so the kite came up a bit. And unfortunately he never stayed up for more than a few seconds...

"Come, I'll show you again!" Arthur's dad flew on the spot. It worked! Arthuro was excited, but the October wind up here was just right for him, and he wore it fantastically.

"Great, Arthur! Just a little more! "The brown-haired boy with the freckles on his nose ran faster than ever. Nevertheless, he wished for a bit more wind. Then it would be even easier. When he looked up at the mountain for a moment, he did not believe his eyes: "Daddy - look! A little dragon is practicing with his daddy! "" Only the flag at the summit cross broke loose ", his dad laughed" Go on, run another round."

Arthuro was flying so safely and happily now that he had almost made it halfway up the mountain. When he saw the boy with the paper kite, he landed behind a pile of stones and watched him curiously. Just that second, the human boy told his dad how nice it would be if his paper kite could fly as well as the little dragon on the mountain. "Yes, yes, my noble knight! Dragons are special animals! And you really have a lot of feelings for her, be it real or paper. "

The little dragon was very happy about the praise and decided to take the boy under the wings. How good that he could not spit fire! He took a deep breath and blew through his nostrils as hard as he could. "Hooray, he's flying!" Arthur was pleased because his paper kite not only stayed in the air, but played well with the wind - depending on how much air Arthuro blew out of his hiding place. "Have fun, little man," he thought. "Maybe we can play together once! After all, you're good and careful with dragons! "

Sleep-travel 28: Mom, who is making the wind?

Lisa goes with her mom to the kindergarten. Lisa is a girl with two little pigtails that hang over her ears day after day. She is also a very funny girl who likes to know everything and therefore often asks many questions. Sometimes there are so many questions, sometimes she finds the answers very difficult. Then she has to come up with an answer herself.

It is a gray morning. "Gray can be different," says Lisa. The adults do not like the gray sky in the fall, they find it boring. Lisa likes to watch gray clouds. She sometimes walks with her head up, keeping her face in the direction of the gray clouds passing by in the sky. She thinks that some clouds look like cuddly animals. Mama always has to laugh about Lisa. But Lisa may just go with her head in the clouds.

, This morning it is especially exciting. The clouds are running a race today. Lisa is watching a small, bright cloud sheep take a lead in front of a large, dark cloud animal. Lisa claps her hands with joy. Mama says: "This is the wind that makes the clouds run so fast in the sky". Lisa stops. She did not think about that. She must immediately think of the fun game they have been doing in kindergarten for a few days. Lisa and other children stand in a circle, holding up their arms, wiggling, blowing with all their might. They have learned that wind moves tree branches.

Then her mum shows a series of brown autumn leaves that magically rise from the ground and spin in the air. "The wind also makes the leaves dance," says Mama. Lisa looks deeply into her mum's face and must quickly ask a question: "Mom, who's doing the wind?"

Again, this is a question to which Mama finds only one difficult answer: "Wind is air that flees from one place to another. She is in a hurry. "Lisa wants to know more precisely:" But who makes the wind? "Mom tries again:" When the air gets warm from the sun, it becomes light and rises. Then cold air comes down, until it gets warm too. So the warm and the cold air volumes always exchange their places. "Before Lisa can ask the next question, Mama finds that they have to hurry to get to kindergarten on time. Lisa moans, then she has to come up with an answer herself.

When they finally arrived in the warm kindergarten, Lisa was suddenly all right. Of course! The air is in a hurry to arrive in a warm place. Lisa could understand that very well.

Conclusion

These tales are relaxing to hear, and perfect for those who need to catch some Z's. with each story, you were whisked away into a far-off place, a dream land where people, places, and things aren't as they seem. Where everything seems almost...surreal in a sense. Understanding that is of course, a great way to understand these stories, putting them all together so that you can hear a great tale, and one that's deep, but also relaxing as well.

With that being said, I hope these tales will help with sleeping. They are whimsical pieces, and they are quite fun. You've heard the many adventures that either put you in the place of the main character, or you heard some fun, interesting stories that you won't want to ever forget. These unforgettable tales will help lure anyone to sleep, no matter how good, or how bad their sleep schedule is.

Just listen to one every night before you go to bed, and you'll go straight to dream and, whisked off by the adventures you hear through the words uttered. So, there you have it, I hope you're able to get yourself some sleep that's worthwhile, and filling.

As you get through life, there are a lot of things that could have transpired during the day, but having a cool and quiet night rest is the best way to recuperate and stay in shape. Nothing compares to memorable bedtime stories in the winter under comfortable spreads. To pay tribute to this prime cuddle climate, the stories herein are specially selected to keep you in ease your anxiety.

The most important goal that I hoped to achieve by authoring this was to allow the reader an easy and effective means to relax. Stories have been created for centuries to allow us to step outside of ourselves. Life can be a real bummer sometimes, and stress is unavoidable. I hope that was able to sweep you away for a little while, to some interesting locations. I wanted to help you build a paradise in your own mind, a realm that you can visit whenever you need to unwind.

Dreams are what dictate how we respond and react in the days that follow. Positive dreams lead us to respond positively. If you're struggling to sleep and desire to find peace, there is no better way to dictate your night than through a bedtime story. Through these stories, you can not only send yourself drifting off to sleep swiftly. By choosing the story that fits your mood best, only you will know, you can lull yourself into the slumber that will match your next day.

With each of these stories, as you hear them when you sleep, you'll notice when you wake up you feel refreshed. That's because, with each sound, you'll hear words as well that are relaxing, soothing, and will help with sleep. Instead of stories that will keep you on your feet and alert, these small, short stories are simple, and yet very effective. If you have trouble relaxing, turning your mind off, and lulling the body to sleep, then this is for you. With each passing story, you'll feel your attention slowly slip away. Each sound you hear pulling you into a far-off land, into a realm of sleep that makes you feel happy, and at ease.

CPSIA information can be obtained
at www.ICGtesting.com
Printed in the USA
LVHW050442251120
672446LV00014B/236